Army Combat Medics
in the Vietnam War

ALSO BY HARRY SPILLER
AND FROM MCFARLAND

*Navy Corpsmen in the Vietnam War:
17 Personal Accounts* (2021)

*The Afghanistan Poppy Eradication Campaign: Accounts
from the Black Hawk Counter-Narcotics Infantry
Kandak Team in Helmand Province* (2017)

*Veterans of Iraq and Afghanistan: Personal Accounts
of 22 Americans Who Served* (2014)

*Scars of Vietnam: Personal Accounts by Veterans
and Their Families* (1994; paperback 2012)

*Death Angel: A Vietnam Memoir of a Bearer of Death
Messages to Families* (1992; paperback 2012)

*Support Programs for Ex-Offenders:
A State-by-State Directory* (2011)

*American POWs in World War II: Twelve Personal
Accounts of Captivity by Germany and Japan* (2009)

*Pearl Harbor Survivors: An Oral History
of 24 Servicemen* (2002)

*American POWs in Korea: Sixteen
Personal Accounts* (1998)

*Prisoners of Nazis: Accounts by American
POWs in World War II* (1998)

Army Combat Medics in the Vietnam War

Nine Personal Accounts

HARRY SPILLER

McFarland & Company, Inc., Publishers
Jefferson, North Carolina

ISBN (print) 978-1-4766-9425-2
ISBN (ebook) 978-1-4766-5206-1

Library of Congress and British Library
cataloguing data are available

© 2024 Harry Spiller. All rights reserved

No part of this book may be reproduced or transmitted in any form or by any means, electronic or mechanical, including photocopying or recording, or by any information storage and retrieval system, without permission in writing from the publisher.

Front cover images: *from top left,* SP-5 John Maag, mountains of Dak To, 1967; SSgt Penn Davidson at Dak To, 1969; SP-5 Neil Keddie in battalion ambulance near Hue; SP-5 Ray Hubbard at Aid Station Dak To Base.

Printed in the United States of America

*McFarland & Company, Inc., Publishers
Box 611, Jefferson, North Carolina 28640
www.mcfarlandpub.com*

Author's Note

The information in this book was obtained through personal interviews, telephone interviews, and written documents. The accounts of the army medics have been minimally edited for grammar and reflect their own words as fully as possible. All illustrations were provided by the individuals. The information in Appendix A came from records of Arlington National Cemetery. The information from Appendix B came from information from the Vietnam War Memorial.

To all Vietnam combat medics of the U.S.
Army and their families.

Acknowledgments

I would like to thank all the Army combat medics who shared their experiences in the Vietnam War. Also, a special thanks to Candice Lahr and Bill and Lisa Cox for their help with research and photos.

Table of Contents

Author's Note — v
Acknowledgments — viii
Introduction — 1

One. SP-5 Michael Guadagno, Quang Nai Province, 1968–69 — 5

Two. SP-5 Richard Pastor, Long Thanh North, 1969–71 — 18

Three. SP-5 Raydon E. Hubbard, Pleiku, An Khe, 1969–70 — 28

Four. SP-4 Leo Flory, I–Corps Area North and West of Hue, 1968–69 — 71

Five. SP-5 William "Neil" Keddie, Jr., Camp Eagle, I Corps, 1969–70 — 106

Six. SP-4 Dwayne Williams, Phu Bai, 1970–71 — 120

Seven. SP-5 James E. Barnes, Dak To, 1967–68 — 126

Eight. SP-5 John M. Maag, Dak To, Pleiku, 1967–68 — 136

Nine. Staff Sergeant Alfred Penn Davidson, Pleiku, January 1969–December 1969 — 150

Appendix A: In Memory — 167
Appendix B: Vietnam Facts and Statistics — 170
Index — 173

Combat Medic Prayer

Oh, Lord I ask for your divine strength to meet the demands of my profession. Help me to be the finest medic, both technically and tactically.

If I am called to the battlefield, give me the courage to conserve our fighting forces by providing medical care to all who are in need.

If I am called to a mission of peace, give me the strength to lead by caring for those who need my assistance.

Finally, Lord help me to take care of my own spiritual, physical, and emotional needs.

Teach me to trust in your presence and never-failing love.
AMEN

Introduction

The Army Medical Service Corps traces its beginning to the American Revolution with the creation of the Ambulance Corps. During the Civil War, the Union Army realized there was a need for an integrated medical treatment and evacuation system. With major developments in World War I, the Medical Services Corp initiated the Sanitary Corps to serve in medical logistics. The onset of World War II inflicted devasting casualties with a lack of medical professionals.

The Army National Guard, Organized Reserves and affiliated medical units from civilian universities moved quickly to provide necessary training to technical personnel, nurses and doctors. Medics were trained with infantry soldiers, learning how to best use the lay of the land for their protection and that of the wounded soldier. The titles of first-aid man, hospital orderly, litter bearer or ambulance driver became part of the classification of Military Occupational Specialty, or MOS 657.

Army combat medics were responsible for evaluation and treatment of wounds and minor injuries. They were trained to make and apply arm or leg splints, bandage wounds, treat patients for shock and stop bleeding by applying tourniquets. They performed routine duties and cleaning that included taking temperatures and pulse readings, bathing and feeding patients and preparing patients for surgical procedures, as well as cleaning and sterilizing specified areas. In addition, they lifted patients onto litters and carried them to aid stations, ambulance loading points or collection stations. The highly respected and easily identified Red Cross symbol on the medic's helmet or arm band became a conspicuous target of enemy snipers. Nevertheless, the combat medic's main objective was to get to the wounded as quickly as possible and move them away from the front line.

During the war, such drugs as sulfa (sulfanilamide) and penicillin were discovered as well as advanced techniques, effectively contributing to the survival rate. A wounded soldier, if treated within the first hour, had an 85 percent chance of survival. Contributing to that survival rate was the speed with which the combat medic on the front line attended to the soldier. At the war's beginning the medics were often ridiculed, sometimes being called "pill pushers," or worse. In combat, however, that attitude drastically changed as they gained respect from all ranks. When a soldier cried out "Medic" there was no hesitation, and they were eventually referred to as "Doc."

The physicians, dentists, nurses and enlisted personnel known as medics cared for 14 million patients during World War II. The Combat Medical Badge (CMB) was introduced on March 3, 1945, for medical personnel who served with detachments during World War II. The badge was designed to provide recognition to the field medic who accompanied the infantryman into battle. According to the Department of the Army, the medic must have been personally present and under fire to be eligible for the CMB.

During the Vietnam War, mandatory deployment lasted one year, with the option to extend. In theory, medics were supposed to spend some of their deployment working in hospitals on the edge of the battlegrounds or slightly farther out and some of it following soldiers into combat. However, they were usually sent wherever they were most needed, which typically meant being attached to a regiment completing missions in the line of fire. In short, they followed their fellow soldiers into brutal battles fought and lost in the impenetrable heat and claustrophobic thickness of the jungle to attend to the wounded. They put their own lives in danger to save those of their fellow soldiers. According to the U.S. Army Department, more than 1,100 medics were killed in Vietnam and 19 medics who served in Vietnam were awarded the Medal of Honor, the nation's highest military honor. Eight of the medals were awarded posthumously.

Unlike in other wars, Vietnam medics carried weapons. Most had an M16A1 rifle, a .45-caliber pistol and grenades. Like the infantrymen, they didn't have body armor or bulletproof helmets. Many times, medics went into battle with very limited supplies, typically as many bandages, gauze rolls and morphine syringes as they could carry or persuade others to carry, and possibly an IV bag and a pair of scissors. The phrase "Band-Aid over a bullet wound" is grimly close to what they were able to accomplish. But the combat medics' purpose was to patch up their fellow soldiers well enough that they could be moved to an area accessible to helicopters.

The use of medevac helicopters to provide in-transport medical care in the Vietnam War saved countless lives. Dustoff missions alone picked up an estimated 900,000 wounded soldiers and Vietnamese civilians during the war. Dustoffs used UH-1 Iroquois helicopters ("Huey") to carry out missions. The Huey had a four-man crew—a pilot, an aircraft commander, a medic and a crew chief. When they landed, the medic and crew chief were responsible for loading the wounded into the back on litters, where they could administer first aid, including blood transfusions and fluids via IVs. The success of this approach has inspired emergency medical responders around the world.

From the battlefield, the wounded would be medevaced to an aid station, which had more resources to deal with severe injuries. From there, the worst cases would be flown on to a remote and better-equipped hospital or even to a ship hospital. Those who recovered were often sent back out to fight again.

Army medics were also responsible for the general health of the soldier. Medics reminded the soldiers to take malaria pills and stay hydrated. A common problem was jungle rot from soldiers having wet feet for long periods of time. Medics constantly reminded soldiers to change socks to keep their feet dry. Dysentery, ring worm and head lice were also a problem. Often sexually transmitted diseases were picked up from brothels and were treated with penicillin shots.

As well as caring for American soldiers, the medics treated South Vietnamese villagers and even prisoners of war. Common treatments were for parasites, tuberculosis, typhoid, dysentery and war-related wounds. The American medical staff also passed on their medical knowledge to Vietnamese doctors and nurses.

When veterans returned home as sentiment in the U.S. turned against the war, the hostile attitudes of American civilians toward them prevented many from finding an outlet. Many were haunted by nightmares, memories of specific incidents or soldiers they'd lost. Many experienced post-traumatic stress disorder and other psychological issues, not to mention long-term effects of chemical weapons like Agent Orange. The medical staff learned to repress their emotions at the time so they could do their jobs. They just had to shut their emotions down. Veterans centers upgraded their sources, and many received therapy and found their way back to civilian life. However, for many the war will never end.

I served in the United States Marine Corps for 10 years, from June 1963 through June 1973. During that time, I did two tours (1965 and 1971–72) in the Vietnam War. One thing that stands out from those experiences is the strong bond between the Navy corpsmen and the Marines. They were our lifeline in combat. The Army combat medic was also the lifeline for soldiers in the field. In general, they don't talk about the lives they saved or the people they helped or the sick they treated. Instead, they talk about the lives they didn't save, the soldiers they couldn't help. For them their actions were never enough; they should have done more. Although they may not have been God, they sure were God-sent for the soldiers in Vietnam.

These experiences are my inspiration for writing this book. There are nine personal accounts of Army combat medics who served in the

Vietnam War. From Dak To in the Northern Highlands to I Corps in Phu Bai and Quang Nai Province, these Army combat medics attended to sick and wounded soldiers and provided medical care for thousands of Vietnamese villagers. Awards among them included the Bronze Star, Vietnamese Cross of Gallantry with Bronze Star, Silver Star, Army Commendation Medal and Purple Heart. Their stories are gripping and often gut-wrenching. However, in their minds they never did enough. There was always one more person they could have helped or one more they could have saved.

ONE

SP-5 Michael Guadagno, Quang Nai Province, 1968–69

4TH BN, 21ST INFANTRY DIVISION, 11TH LIB AMERICAL DIVISION

Vietnam Campaign Medal, Vietnam Service Medal, Combat Medical Badge, Air Medal, Vietnam Cross of Gallantry Medal, Army Commendation Medal, National Defense Service Medal, Good Conduct Medal

I have been contemplating telling my story for quite a few years but never did because of what a "hot button" issue the Vietnam War was. We were shunned by American society and told to blend in and not mention what we did over there or even admit to being there. We were flown into the United States under the cover of darkness and told not to wear our uniforms home because most people would react negatively or even violently. I spent the better part of 40-plus years immersed in my work and raising a family. Vietnam seemed like it never happened. If the subject came up, it was quickly dropped. It was *not* something to be proud of … as we were convinced by society. I think society has finally realized the last few years what a travesty this treatment was and today it is generally accepted, and people even apologize for our treatment. That's all in the past and cannot be "undone," but at least I feel like I can now be proud of the role I played. As we [Vietnam vets] always say, "We were winning when I left." I proudly display my colors and am most proud of the Combat Medical Badge I earned helping my brothers to survive. Everyone had a job and that was mine.

As these memories are from almost 50 years ago, I cannot remember dates so none will be listed and hopefully the chronological order is correct. I am going to refrain from using names of the injured and dead because I feel it is too sensitive an issue in case their family members were to read this.

I entered the U.S. Army on May 20, 1968. Took basic training at Fort Jackson, South Carolina, for eight weeks. Sent to Fort Sam Houston for army medic training for 10 weeks. I had my 20th birthday/going-away party on October 31, 1968, and was on my way to Vietnam on November 5. Arrived Cam Ran Bay and immediately sent to Chu Lai (I Corp) for in-country processing/ training.

I remember one of my first duties in Chu Lai was shit-burning detail. You had to gather up the half-55-gallon drums from the back of the crappers, take them to the edge of the perimeter and pour diesel fuel in them and burn and stir and stir and stir. The smell was putrid. This was one of those duties they gave FNGs (fucking new guys). We slept on cots in wooden hooches, and the sides were piled high with sandbags but the roofs were corrugated tin. I thought this was hell, but little did I know what was in store.

After about a week, I was sent down to LZ Bronco by the town of Duc Pho in the Quang Nai Province, headquarters of the American Division and the Jungle Warriors. Not as big a place as Chu Lai but the accommodations were about the same. I was attached to HHC of the 4th Battalion, 21st Infantry Division, 11th Light Infantry Brigade, Medical Company. I soon found out that these accommodations were also temporary as all medics were required to spend at least six months out in the "field." I thought this was the field. Oh, no, I wasn't even close to the "field."

I spent about a week getting oriented and gathering up all the necessary items that a "grunt medic" would need out in the field. Aid bag, rucksack, C rations, bedding, extra bandages, ammunition, M-16, hand grenades, smoke grenades, poncho and liner, etc. I soon learned that I would become much more efficient at what was "necessary" and what was not. Humping close to 100 pounds was not fun and you did without whatever you could, such as for shelter we snapped together poncho liners. Air mattresses were useless as they might last you a week if you were lucky. Medics were *not* required to carry a weapon, but I opted to carry an M-16 rather than a .45 cal. or nothing.

It was during Vietnam's monsoon, and I was trying to catch a Huey to get out to forward Fire Support Base Amy in the mountains. After about three days of trying, I finally got a ride on a Chinook. I landed at LZ Amy (high in the mountains) and jumped off the back of the Chinook and sank up to my ankles in mud. I reported into the base aid station and was told to find a bunker to sleep in and report back in the morning. I slept on some C ration boxes laid on top of mud but was at least out of the rain. These accommodations really sucked and could not get much worse (little did I know). The next morning I was told I needed to get on a Huey and join my company "in the bush." I thought this *was* the bush.

One. Michael Guadagno

I piled onto a Huey with about five other guys, no doors and M60 machine gunners on both sides, and held on for dear life as we flew to a small mountain ridge a few miles away where my Company "C" (Charlie) was set up for RON (rest over night). They popped red smoke, and the chopper came close to landing ... about 10 feet off the ground. I didn't want to jump but they threatened me so I pretty much fell out and got all scraped up. I got up and dusted myself off and found my lieutenant and introduced myself as his new medic

SP-5 Michael Guadagno after medic training at Fort Sam Houston in San Antonio, Texas.

and excused myself to attend to my injuries. What a grand entrance. From then on, I was paired up usually with the RTO (radio telephone operator) whose name was Hud (cannot remember his real name). I was told I would be the CP (command platoon) medic as well as 1st Platoon medic because they were short of medics. I was paired up with someone because at night we would snap together our ponchos to act as a sort of tent. Sometimes we would snap together many ponchos, depending on how many trees were available to tie to. From here the chronological order gets really hazy. I can remember some events and some details but there are lots of pieces and faces missing, but I will try to fill in as many blanks as I can.

As a medic you were responsible for your guys' health and well-being. You gave out salt tabs every day and malaria pills. Had an informal sick call and tended to all sorts of injuries and illnesses. I carried an aid bag full of bandages, tape, morphine, aspirin, Darvon, surgical kit, scissors, cravat, airway, etc. It was *always* with me.

I remember the leeches (during monsoon season). They would latch onto you and suck your blood and leave an anticoagulant, then drop off when they were full, and you would continue bleeding. You had to be careful, or the wound would get infected. I always had a few pairs of shoelaces crisscrossed from my boots up to my knees to keep the leeches out

Michael Guadagno (center) and a couple of medics cutting up in the aid station at LZ Bronco.

of my pants. The shoelaces also came in handy as a tourniquet to stop bleeding when limbs were lost (used them more than a few times). I used Army-issued mosquito repellant to keep the leeches off the rest of my body. The stuff did not work on mosquitoes, but the leeches hated it (thank God).

I woke up one morning in the bush and when I got out of my hooch, Hud (our RTO) looked at me in horror and said, "WTF happened to you, Doc?" I didn't know what he was talking about, so he threw me a mirror from the survival kit and said, "Look." My entire face was covered in blood. Apparently, a leech had taken up residence on my lip, fed and dropped off, and I thought it was sweat and continued to wipe my face with my hands in my sleep, spreading the blood all over. We had a good laugh.

In the morning we all did our chores, packed up and prepared for the day's "hump." That's what we called hiking because we humped all this crap on our backs all over Vietnam. Sometimes 15–20 klicks before we set up RON. Depending on whether we were in the mountains or the rice paddies or plains.

It was around Christmas (1968), and we were setting up on a mountaintop and received sniper fire. My lieutenant (Ricci) called in for artillery and/or air support but was denied because we were under a Christmas cease-fire. Who told the snipers? What a joke! The lieutenant was told not to return fire or engage. He informed the rear that their transmission was breaking up and could not hear them. He then instructed us to return fire. This was probably my first taste of the politics of war.

Seems to me that we humped for a couple of months with not much action but one day coming down out of the mountains, our point man was confronted by two NVA (North Vietnamese Army) regulars and killed one but the other guy got away. We were concerned and rightfully so. The NVA that we killed had American Army-issued mosquito repellant and a bayonet, and a GI's camera. Probably from a GI he had killed (we surmised). Little did we know that this was the beginning of us stepping into "shit" every time we turned around. No more peace and quiet.

We went out into this plains/rice paddy area just outside of Duc Pho and got ambushed by some NVA and it was utter chaos because they were yelling and we were yelling and the helicopter gunships were trying to provide air support and every time we popped smoke to give our position the chopper pilots would see two smokes because the VC were trying to confuse them. We finally won the skirmish. Seems to me we had a few injuries, but I don't remember any casualties … but wait.

Michael Guadagno in Vietnam, 1968.

The brass back at the base camp decided that there were probably a company of NVA and some VC in that area and they sent scout dogs and APCs (armored personnel carriers or tracks) out to support us. I hated the tracks because they were so noisy and seemed to attract RPGs (rocket-propelled grenades) and when those suckers hit a track, there was shrapnel flying everywhere.

We were reconning the area when one of the scout dogs came on point to a hedgerow. As our company advanced, an NVA with a Chicom (Chinese communist) machine gun opened fire on us and a few guys went down. They started yelling for a medic. My buddy Sammy (also a medic) and I took off toward the hedgerow and I can remember thinking that this was like one of those Audie Murphy movies with bullets whizzing and dirt being kicked up as we ran toward the machine gun. I thought I was insane. I grabbed my aid bag with one hand and M16 with the other and fired back while we ran. Sammy hit the deck behind a rice paddy dyke first and as I came in after him, my left foot felt like it had been slapped out from under me and I thought I was hit. I told Sammy and he looked and said, "Holy shit, your boot sole has been cut in half." We were pinned down and could not get to the wounded without committing suicide. It was *sure* death. Which is exactly what happened to one of the other medics, who came in running from the front left side. As he got to the wounded, he was hit in the head, and I can remember seeing his head exploding like a watermelon. I was horrified and scared to death. We finally had to get the tracks up with us and approach the hedgerow and machine gunner using the tracks as cover. Most of the guys hit were dead. Some of our guys (I believe Fred was one of them) took out the machine gunner and we were able to get control.

Later that night we set up a perimeter and in the middle of the night we started receiving small-arms fire and mortar rounds dropping inside the perimeter. I heard someone yelling "Medic" and I left my M16 and ran to a foxhole and jumped in. I will never forget the smell and horrific sight of what a person had once been, all blown apart and burning flesh and meat everywhere. Two guys were in the foxhole, and one had taken a direct hit, the other was moaning and rocking back and forth and was full of shrapnel holes all over his body. All I could think about was that they hit this hole once and probably would again. I wrapped up the other guy as best I could and tried dragging him out of the foxhole, but he was too big for me to handle. I finally got help to get him out. We got control of the situation after losing about half our company to injuries or casualties. Thank God for the Shark and Cobra gunships. The smell of *death* was everywhere. The next morning, they evacuated us, and we later found out that we went up against a *battalion*, not a *company* of NVA. We were

Entrance back at the base camp, LZ Bronco at Duc Pho.

seriously outmanned. We loaded the wounded on medevacs first and then the dead later. My M16 got sent in with the dead bodies. I couldn't wait to get it back.

Since we had lost so many men, the brass decided to put us on forward firebase duty (bunker guard) until they could get us back up to strength. Sounded like a good idea ... right? Nope! They sent us to LZ Amy. After a few days we were hit one night and got sappers inside the perimeter. These guys were highly trained NVA or VC that got inside your defenses and created chaos in advance of other ground forces. They forced you to fight a war in two different directions. From within and without. There were explosions and small-arms fire everywhere. I was in a bunker and saw a VC heading down the hill. He looked at me and I leveled my weapon and fired ... but it jammed. Glad he decided to keep going because it took a bit to unjam the damn thing. We repelled the attack but in all the commotion and weapon firing the ammo dump (full of 105, 155, M79, M60, 81 MM and M16 rounds) caught on fire. We were pinned down for what seemed like three days or so until the rounds stopped exploding, some flying into the air and some exploding harmlessly on the ground. We could not have resupply or any choppers in the vicinity until the rounds quit exploding. During the fight, one of the sappers got into our TOC (tactical operations center). This was where the brass was located and all our communication equipment. One of our guys that was on TOC watch (guard) had a sapper jump down off the roof, directly in front of him, and the sapper fired his weapon and hit him in the front of the helmet. Somehow the round hit a glancing blow and knocked him out. He had a hole in his helmet but not his head (thank God). The sapper was killed by another guard. We were doing recon on the hill for dead enemy, and we noticed that the 55-gallon drums from one of the crappers had been pulled out, so we opened the flap and found a dead enemy. This guy was every bit of six feet tall and had more body hair than your typical Vietnamese. He appeared to everyone to be Chinese. Hmm. A few nights after the attack and we were scheduled to go out into the field the next day. One of the guys decided he was not going to go, and he took his M16 and shot himself in the lower leg. The bullet hit the bone and traveled down and came out his ankle. I gave him a shot of morphine, bandaged him up and called for medevac. Thank God the remainder of our time on LZ Amy was quiet and we returned to the field.

    They had us out in Quang Nai Province patrolling the AO (area of operation) and our colonel (Donaldson, I believe) said he saw a North Vietnam flag flying in a village nearby and wanted us to go in and take it down. We all knew what that meant. The place was booby trapped! We were told to stay off paths and be aware of anything strange. I was so afraid I was actually walking *through* hedgerows. I didn't care, I was not going to step foot on any paths. We hadn't been in there long and I heard an explosion and then the cry for "Medic." I took off running, hoping not to get blown up myself, and when I got to my guys, there were what seemed to be about 10 guys with various injuries all over the place. I tried to assess the most serious and that seemed to a guy lying under a tree with the back of his head blown off and he was swallowing his tongue and it didn't look good. I forced an airway into his mouth and gave him some morphine for pain and moved to the next injured. It was bad. Guys lost eyes and limbs. We did the best we could and got them medevacked. Apparently, there was an explosive device in a tree with a trip wire that was tripped. The man with the most serious injury was one of our medics. The village was *vacant*. We took the flag down.

    We moved on to another old forward firebase that had been vacated a while back. I believe it was called LZ Dragon. We were tasked with securing it and helping to reopen it. Guess what. It was also booby trapped. At first it was quiet. We surveyed the area and started to settle in and even were able to have a resupply chopper come in and bring sundries and mail. One of the guys had gotten a package from home with some cookies in it and about four of us were walking down the hill to share his cookies when one of the guys next to me stepped on a Bouncing Betty. The thing exploded out of the ground, sent dirt everywhere and hit the guy in the knee and rolled off harmlessly into an old bunker. The guy that stepped on it was in real bad pain and it appeared he at least had a broken knee. These Bouncing Betties are supposed to be propelled into the air at about

One. Michael Guadagno

Guadagno and his guys found a cache of weapons. They searched the village looking for weapons and large supplies of rice.

three feet high and then explode, sending shrapnel everywhere. I'm sure I and others would probably be dead today if not for it hitting directly into his knee. I gave him some morphine and bandaged him up and medevaced him.

We finally got the perimeter set up and got some artillery flown in and we started firebase bunker watch. A couple of nights later we got sappers in the perimeter again and they raised hell and killed a bunch of guys. I was confronted with my first sucking chest wound during the skirmish. We were trained how to deal with these things in that you tore off the plastic from the field dressing and threw the bandage away and put the plastic over the hole and put tape around the perimeter of the plastic, making an airtight seal so the lung would not suck in any more air. I tried this but the one thing they did not tell us is that it is impossible to get the tape to stick with all that blood. I could do nothing else but hold my hand over it and try to keep it airtight. Luckily, we had a doctor on the hill and I was able to get him to the medical convex with some help. While there the doctor wanted some of us medics to assist with some of the more seriously wounded. I remember one guy lying on the stretcher and his leg was just mangled. The doctor wanted to put an air splint on his leg to help control the bleeding and also to immobilize and set the leg. I was at the end of the stretcher and the doctor asked me to pull on his leg when they gave me the signal. "Just grab the toe and heel and give it a good pull and don't let go."

I did but the doctor yelled for me to pull harder. I did and it felt like the leg moved at least six inches toward me. It was a sickening feeling.

A few days later the guys in the field captured a VC that had been burned by napalm. He was black and pink all over and having lots of difficulty breathing. The doctor said he was going to show us how to do a field tracheotomy like they had showed us in medical training. He took a church key (can opener) and took the ends and insides out of a ball point pen and punched a hole in the guy's trachea and inserted the pen and taped it in place. He was breathing but died a short time later.

Back out to the field again. This time with the Tracks also. (Did I say I hated them?) We were out patrolling and one of our FNGs (fucking new guy) stepped on a booby trap and it blew off both his legs from the knee down. There were slivers of bone sticking out. I used my shoelaces as a tourniquet and controlled the bleeding and medevaced him. We set up RON that night and we came under attack by RPGs (rocket-propelled grenades). We called in gunships and repelled the attack. Some KIA on our side and wounded. Goodbye to the Tracks.

While setting up another RON one night, I heard what sounded like a "bloop" from an M79 grenade launcher but not followed by an explosion. I heard "Medic" and ran over to find that one of our guys was cleaning his M79 trigger mechanism and had the barrel resting on his hip bone and he had a live round in the chamber and when he slammed the stock shut it triggered the round and it fired and lodged against his hip bone. It didn't explode because it was not armed until it had gone at least 30 meters. I bandaged him, gave him morphine and called for medevac. The medic on board asked what was wrong and I told him he had a live M79 grenade against his hip. I said to not rotate him too much as it might arm the grenade. A little medic humor, but true.

We moved up into the mountains and one night while we were setting up our RON we heard an explosion and guys started yelling "Incoming." We hit the deck but there was nothing else. Then guys started yelling "Medic." Apparently, some of the guys snuck off in the bush and smoked up some weed and one of them decided to play hot potato with a live grenade. It went off, obviously, and I think one was KIA and a few wounded. How stupid.

That night we received sniper fire so we called in the gunships, and they peppered the area and dropped flares so we could see. We repelled the attack, and the next morning found some dead VC as well as parts of fingers fused to the plastic casing on a claymore mine cover. It appeared that one of the VC was in the process of trying to turn the mine around on us when one of us set it off, toasting him in the process.

Humping back down toward the lowlands, one of the guys discovered what appeared to be a booby trap buried on the trail. Our captain decided he was going to detonate it himself because he had been trained in this. He probed at it and finally decided to set it off with a hand grenade. He told all of us to take cover and he pulled the pin and placed the grenade gently and let the spoon fly and took cover behind a big rock. Problem was that he was such a tall guy, his legs were still exposed, and he took shrapnel in his shins. He wasn't wounded too bad but could not hump with us anymore. The colonel's Charlie (command chopper) was in the area and decided to land and take Captain back to LZ Bronco. I guess on the way back they buzzed some VC farmers and one of them threw a hoe up and hit the chopper tail rotor and the chopper went down. We now had to go and secure the chopper and provide a perimeter for the passengers.

LZ Bronco had been getting rocket attacks off and on for quite a few days, so they decided to send us up the side of this hill that they thought the rockets were being launched from. As luck would have it, as we were heading up the side of this hill, the enemy launched a rocket. We called in their position and requested F4 Phantom support. The first pass was a strafing run using his onboard cannon but the pilot had our coordinates wrong and came in right over us. His ejected shells started falling down through the trees and hitting guys. They were hot and could do damage if they hit you wrong. We called him off and he came in from a different direction. The rocket site was destroyed.

I remember one day while I was back at the base camp. Our commanding officer volunteered me to be the medic for a group of about seven LRRPS (long-range reconnaissance patrols) that was to be dropped off at night to monitor the movements of some NVA in the area. I remember sitting on a hillside waiting for some signs of enemy so we could report. I was scared shitless because there were so few of us. Thank God we did not make any contact and were extracted the next day.

By this time, I had finished my seven months in the bush and was reassigned back to LZ Bronco. I hated this duty because it was spit-shine boots and full fatigue uniforms and just too much military crap. I volunteered for forward firebase duty and was sent to LZ Charlie Brown, and I ran a one-man aid station for a four deuce mortar platoon that was providing fire support for the I Corps area around Quang Nai Province and the town of Sa Huyn.

I finished up about four months on this firebase and received a seven-day drop, which meant I was going home seven days early. If this was true, it would mean I would be home for my 21st birthday. I processed out of LZ Bronco and flew down to Cam Ranh Bay to catch a flight home. As luck would have it, I spent my seven days in Cam Ranh Bay and celebrated my birthday at the NCO club because they were receiving rocket

Michael Guadagno eating some C rations in the bush at one of his many overnight accommodations.

attacks and the planes could not land or take off. They also had to repair the runway.

I finally got out of Vietnam after *exactly* one year and flew on (I believe) a Flying Tiger. The plane was quiet as a church mouse until we felt we were clear of Vietnam airspace, then everyone erupted into chants of "Fuck Vietnam." We had made it.

I had heard about some of the protesting going on back home but when we landed under cover of darkness at McChord Air Force Base, we were shuffled off to an orientation of sorts. We were told *not* to wear our uniforms home on leave and *not* to discuss our military experiences. The American public was not receiving us well. What the *hell* did we go over there for? I was really bitter for a long time and just put my Vietnam service and experiences in the back of my mind and pretended like they never happened. Were we to be ashamed that we even went there? I was proud of the service I performed as a combat medic, but I couldn't even show it. *How sad.*

I still had about 18 months to finish my three-year commitment and after my 30 days' leave, I was sent to Fort Bliss, Texas, to finish my enlistment. I was the medical section chief for an artillery outfit until my enlistment ended, May 1971.

Forty years later, after I retired from working, all these memories came flooding back but it seems just the ones that terrified me. I sought help from the VA and was diagnosed with PTSD and began counseling. It helped somewhat but I am still dealing with memories that no one should ever have. I learned that I should be proud of my service and especially proud of my service as a combat medic. My most prized possession is my CMB (Combat Medical Badge). It means I rendered aid to my brothers while under enemy fire.

Two

SP-5 Richard Pastor, Long Thanh North, 1969–71

197th Medical Detachment, 212th Aviation Battalion, 1st Aviation Brigade

Bronze Star, Air Medal, National Defense, Army Commendation Medal, Vietnam Campaign Medal, Vietnamese Gallantry Cross, Vietnamese Civil Action Medal

I was a student at the University of New Hampshire (UNH) from 1964 to January 1969, having been nine credits short of graduation as a chemistry major. I could remember asking for special permission of the registrar to be deferred for the fall 1968 semester if I took an extra course so I could be full-time for that last semester (12 credits needed for full-time status), thus being deferred from the draft.

While in school there were a number of demonstrations against the war, but I had no opinion or participation. The leaders seemed to be hippie types who did not fit the mold of my fraternity brothers, so I never got involved, figuring if the country thought a war was necessary I would serve, as did my father. No way was Canada ever a consideration or thought.

My father was a prisoner of war after the Battle of the Bulge. We all knew that growing up but did not know until a few years before his death that he was placed at a special camp for Jewish prisoners after being separated from the rest of the troops. He was one of the 25 percent who survived that camp and was eventually compensated in the early 2000s by the German government. He never spoke to me or any of the family about his experience, even as I was leaving for the service and later in Vietnam. There were a few books subsequently written about his unit's service, and it was not until then that we all learned the trauma he survived.

For the summer of 1968, I got a job at the General Electric plant in Somersworth, New Hampshire, in the lab. I continued working through

Two. Richard Pastor

the fall 1968 semester while completing my courses at night. Following my graduation in January 1969, I was promoted to a salaried position working with a group called Advanced Development. I thought at the time working at General Electric would be my career. I can remember the conversation, if you could call it that, with the manager at the time when he promoted me to the salaried position. He talked and I listened and could not get a word in edgewise. He was so pleased he was giving me a salary, about $7,500 a year, that he had forgotten he had raised my hourly salary at the end of the summer, so my position resulted in a $5-a-week raise. As he was talking and ushering me out of the office, the final word was "Congratulations."

I worked at GE until I was drafted. I was inducted a week after the first landing on the moon, on July 28, 1969. I went to Fort Dix in New Jersey for eight weeks of basic training. Nothing special happened at basic training, I was just one of the troops. However, everyone knew the chances of going to Vietnam were very high.

After basic training I was shipped to Fort Sam Houston in San Antonio, Texas, for medic school. We learned how to treat wounds and all the ins and outs of being a medic, but one of the things I always laughed about was that they only trained us to work on wounds on the right side. No one had an answer for it. While I was in medic school, I tried to get my MOS changed to a lab technician, as I was a chemistry graduate, but that didn't work out. While in San Antonio, my college roommate and wife came to visit me once and I later spent a weekend at his place in Laredo as he was going through Air Force flight training. He had been ROTC in college. I opted out.

When I graduated, I was surprised to hear I was one of 20 in a class of 665, graduating December 5, 1969, as an honor graduate as a result of written test scores and PT scores.

SP-5 Richard Pastor's graduation from basic training, 1970.

I was never very good in the PT area but always managed to pass. I came to find out somehow the PT scores were all faked and for the first time finished in the upper 75 percent. After graduation I came home on leave and then flew out to Oakland, California, for processing out to Vietnam.

On our flight to Vietnam, we stopped in Hawaii and Wake Island for refueling, but it didn't matter because we could never leave the gate area while the plane was refueling. We landed in Vietnam on January 7, 1970. I then went to the assignment area at Bien Hao. It was packed with guys waiting for orders, which usually took two to four days. We had formation twice a day waiting for assignment. After almost six months in the service, I knew never to volunteer and to certainly never stand in the front row. To this day I am amazed there were guys in the front row. Front rows always get assigned KP or some other shit duty.

Eventually I was assigned to the First Aviation Division, 210th Combat Air Command, 197th Medical Detachment at the Long Thanh North airfield. This was a field about 40 miles west from Saigon about halfway to Vung Tau on the coast, which I never got to see. Long Thanh was a couple miles from Bearcat, a large Air Cav Base and Thai special forces base. There were two other guys who arrived there the same time I did, Greg Antonovich from Massachusetts and Mouse from Kansas, I think. I forgot his name. We were shortly joined by Sam Montgomery from Greenville, South Carolina, and Billy, can't remember his last name, from somewhere in the South. We roomed together and hung out. Also, I remember Ed Mitchell but not sure where he was from.

Overall, there were six to eight medics, an NCO and two doctors running the medical detachment. Dr. Curran, CPT, and Dr. Franco, MAJ, were cool. One was commanding officer for the detachment and the other was commanding officer of the CAC medical wing, so each could sign passes and give us days off. They worked well together. Prior to my leaving, Dr. Franco rotated with no replacement.

We were all required to take a night on rotation to stay at the dispensary to handle emergencies. No guard duty, just be available on rotation for night watch. My very first night in Long Thanh, my very first patient was an unconscious female. I was all thumbs. She was not injured on the right side for one, no blood anywhere, but was breathing. While I was thinking about what to do, NCOIC Tebo came by to check things out. He took over and I was glad I was no longer responsible for her. I don't remember what the issue was, but she ended up being okay.

Normally we did routine sick call duties for all the units on the airfield. I specialized in the lab, drawing on my chemistry background again. We did tests for gonorrhea mostly, but also hepatitis and other things. I gave a lot of shots in the ass and even a few in the arm. The first week we had a mortar attack with everyone grabbing their M-16s and heading for a bunker. This happened occasionally, but not enough to stop regular activities as each event was only one or two mortars. The second or third weekend I was there we were asked if anyone wanted to head to the beach. Not a hard decision as we had lots of planes on the base, and one took the weekly mail run to some island off the coast and flew us to the beach for a day.

On Sunday, February 1, we were all hanging around and there was armed action on the road. Three or four of us jumped in the ambulance and went out to see how we could help, and we got the killed and wounded. Turns out a jeep with contractors was hit by an RPG. While others said they heard gunfire as we picked up the people, I never heard anything. I was too busy focusing on getting the wounded in the ambulance. A few months later I received a Bronze Star with a Combat V. After a somewhat exciting first month we tried to just keep our heads down. I can remember sitting down and writing to a friend that it seemed so unreal. Shot at one day, beach the next in Vietnam.

The first six months I was there I did a lot of drinking, then finally backed off and started counting the days. As we were a detachment, we did not have to play army with the CAC very often. At one point the NCOIC changed and the new SSG was not a medic, just an older lifer who never heard of no formations. We did them for a couple of weeks until he figured out no one cared.

Things were busy at sick call most days and the days were pretty routine. I was involved in all kinds of treatment. I assisted in delivering babies of Vietnamese villagers. I had one guy who had been bitten in the balls by a rat in the latrine and thought for sure he had rabies. He had every textbook symptom, but it was all in his head. Had some serious wounds with a chain saw accident and broken bones. We would treat as best we could and then fly them out to the hospital. Had a suicide or accidental shot in the head of a sergeant. I flew in a chopper to the hospital with him. Had one guy on the way back from Bearcat shot seven times by a little kid.

I had an accident on the road while I was driving back from Bien Hao. We were coming back from the laundry that day and picked up some of the local workers for some reason. It was hard to live down sitting in the driver's seat as the ambulance was towed back by a truck that had a load of hooch girls in it. One crazy day, we had an accident of civilians on a highway with numerous injuries. I can remember that some of the other service members with us were amazed at how us medics could move so fast. We also had a two-engine plane that landed and had forgot to put the landing gear down. Some were injured in that accident. Then one night we finally got a first-run movie in the club. It was *M*A*S*H*. The club reserved the front row for us. The next morning sick call was a bit crazy. We were all

```
                    HEADQUARTERS 1ST AVIATION BRIGADE
                         APO San Francisco 96384

GENERAL ORDERS                  "NGUY HIEM"                    11 June 1970
NUMBER   4927

                    AWARD OF THE BRONZE STAR MEDAL FOR HEROISM

        TC 439. The following AWARDS are announced.

Awarded:      Bronze Star Medal with "V" Device
Date of service: 1 February 1970
Theater:      Republic of Vietnam
Authority:    By direction of the President under the provisions of Executive
              Order 11046, 24 August 1962, AR 672-5-1 and USARV Reg 672-1 dated
              1 July 1969.
Reason:       For heroism in connection with military operations against a hostile
              force: These men distinguished themselves by exceptionally valorous
              actions when a jeep carrying three American civilians was ambushed
              by an unknown size enemy force. These men were immediately dispatched
              to the ambush site to assist in the extraction of the civilians. Upon
              arrival, the rescue party immediately came under a heavy volume of
              hostile automatic weapons fire. With complete disregard for their
              personal safety, they made their way immediately to the wounded
              civilians and carried them to cover. During the entire operation they
              were under constant automatic weapons fire but they did not stop to
              think of their personal safety. Their courage and devotion to duty
              were instrumental in the success of the rescue mission. Their action
              were in keeping with the highest traditions of the military service a
              reflect great credit upon themselves, their units, and the United
              States Army.

AGUIRRE, JIMMY  465-84-7281  STAFF SERGEANT  United States Army
  Headquarters and Headquarters Company, 210th Aviation Battalion (Combat),
  APO 96530
BRISBANE, TIMOTHY W.  172-42-7888  SPECIALIST FIVE  United States Army
  Headquarters and Headquarters Company, 210th Aviation Battalion (Combat),
  APO 96530
MITCHELL, EDWARD M.  379-50-8585  SPECIALIST FIVE  United States Army
  Headquarters and Headquarters Company, 210th Aviation Battalion (Combat),
  APO 96530
NIXON, JOHN R.  165-36-1006  PRIVATE FIRST CLASS  United States Army
  2nd Signal Detachment (Avion), APO 96530
PASTOR, RICHARD L.  002-34-0919  SPECIALIST FOUR  United States Army
  197th Medical Detachment, APO 96530

FOR THE COMMANDER:


OFFICIAL:                              JOSEPH B. STARKER
                                       Colonel, Infantry
                                       Chief of Staff
```

Richard Pastor's Bronze Star Citation.

using the lines from the movie but the guys from the other side of the base hadn't seen the movie and were a bit taken aback.

I also had flight status. That meant flying twice a month for a day. Mostly fixed-wing Beaver, Otter, or two-engine exec transportation planes (eight seats) and flew all over the country as crew chief. We delivered the

Letter of appreciation to Richard Pastor from Donald E. Evon.

mail, supplies, and VIPs to a lot of places. Sometimes landing on just a road and waving at the Air America crews. One day we stopped up north, I forgot where. After the long ride I headed to the latrine. So, there I am standing there and look around and it was all generals who had come for a meeting. I didn't know whether to zip or salute. I zipped and got out of there fast. We stopped at an Aussie base one day. It was very nice. Gave us mess kits for lunch buffet style. The base was in the woods and gave me a picnic feeling.

We ate most meals with the next unit over from us on the base, some Army Security Agency unit. They signed one or two medics from that unit who had special training and worked with us. Their mess hall was much better than ours, so we went there every day for all our meals. Even the doctors came with us a lot. One time we found two ducks hanging around. So, with a grill in place, we quickly decided on grilled duck for dinner. Of course, no one wanted to be the one to slaughter the ducks; finally our CI did the deed. We had the only refrigerator around. We traded lots of good grades on health inspections for cases of steaks. We had a lot of cookouts.

Citation

BY DIRECTION OF THE PRESIDENT

THE AIR MEDAL

IS PRESENTED TO

SPECIALIST FIVE RICHARD L. PASTOR   002-34-0919

who distinguished himself by meritorious achievement, while participating in sustained aerial flight, in support of combat ground forces in the Republic of Vietnam. During the period

5 APRIL 1970 TO 18 JANUARY 1971

he actively participated in more than twenty-five aerial missions over hostile territory in support of operations against communist aggression. During all of these flights, he displayed the highest order of air discipline and acted in accordance with the best traditions of the service. By his determination to accomplish his mission, in spite of the hazards inherent in repeated aerial flights over hostile territory, and by his outstanding degree of professionalism and devotion to duty, he has brought credit upon himself, his organization, and the United States Army.

Richard Pastor's Air Medal Citation.

In April 1970, they had the Cambodia invasion, and we were on edge figuring we were TDY any day, but we never had to go. Also, at the same time was the Kent State shooting, which none of us understood. In December 1970 on Christmas Day, I got to see Bob Hope at Bien Hoa. Somewhere during those months, I did R&R in Taipei and Bangkok. I don't remember who I went with, if anyone. As I was not in an imminent dangerous situation, I extended 60 days to return to the U.S. with less than 150 days and an early out. It worked out fine for me. The last picture of me in uniform was sitting on a garbage can in Oakland, California.

I returned to work at GE after leaving the Army but found my position, and others at that level, had been eliminated. Since they were required

SP-5 Richard Pastor in front of the aid station at Long Thanh North, 1971.

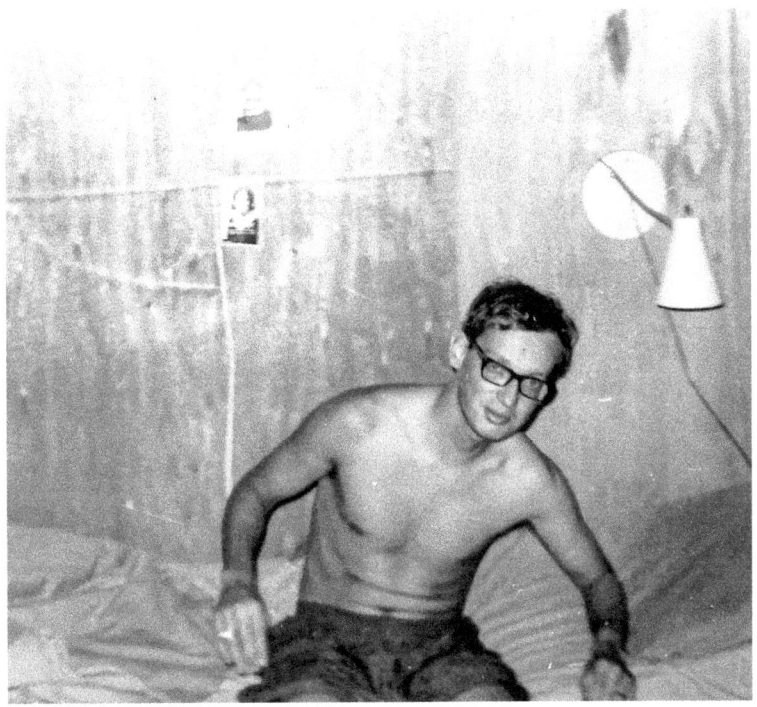

SP-5 Richard Pastor in his living quarters at Long Thanh North, 1971.

to reinstate me in an equal position, I was once again placed in the lab. To do so, one of my friends had to be transferred to the production line. I always felt bad about that. Now that I was no longer in a salaried position, I did not want to stay at GE, so I applied to UNH for the master's program. I used all of my GI Bill education allowance to complete a master of business administration at UNH and an ED in education administration from the University of Massachusetts at Amherst.

I married my wife, Sandy, and had two children, Dawn, who is living in the Houston area, and Dina, who lives in Pelham, NH. I have five grandchildren. I worked for over 40 years in higher education, at two community colleges in Massachusetts and at Daytona State College in Daytona Beach, Florida. Overall, I have always felt a bit guilty when hearing others talk about their Vietnam experiences as I did not do "bush" duty and was not in a daily situation where danger existed. In fact, I never fired a shot but carried an M-16 when off base.

I just received disability award of 30 percent for myasthenia gravis (nerves and muscles not talking to each other) after trying for three years. There is almost no literature on the causal relationship with Agent Orange, but it was approved finally. I started to look into it after six months in the hospital on a respirator, stomach tube, and tracheotomy. I also applied for disability for tinnitus and hearing loss. I have a hearing aid from the VA. I never knew that I could have received medical care from the VA as I always had private insurance. While I support our troops in any way, I do not agree with free medical care for life unless there is disability involved. Even 10 percent disability should qualify, but a healthy person should not

Richard and Sandy Pastor today.

automatically receive full care until a service-related disability or disease surfaces. On November 14, 2022, my disability went to 70 percent. One final note: I cannot stand the sight of blood, even in the movies. Not a pretty picture when I have to be in the hospital.

Three

SP-5 Raydon E. Hubbard, Pleiku, An Khe, 1969–70

4th Infantry Division, 1st Division, 8th Regiment, HHC/Delta Company
Combat Medical Badge and Bronze Star

I arrived at Oakland processing center March 7, 1969, with brand-new "How to be a doctor" skills (10 weeks of AIT—Advanced Individual Training) at Fort Sam Houston. Met up with AIT roomy Bob Hardison from Donaldson, Tennessee. Tons of guys getting sifted and sorted, waiting in lines. Bob and I made the same list every time one was called. I was a PFC at the time.

On March 10, 1969, Flying Tiger Airlines stopped in Hawaii. I called Cousin Arlene during our 45-minute layover. (She was stationed there with her Navy husband, Bill.) She and her two kids, Goosey and Saucy, came to the airport to say hi. Evidently, Hawaii is kind of small and they lived across the street from the airport. Next stop was Wake Island. Holy crap, it's a small island. The runway was about as long and when standing on it, it seemed you could see water in any direction. I think we had to back the plane up just to take off again. The last stop before Vietnam was the Philippines. Clark AFB, probably. Our commercial flight attendants bid us farewell, and I thought what chickens*its. I actually began thinking I was going to have to fight my way off this damn plane when we get there. But a new civilian crew replaced them.

We arrived at Bien Hoa late that night. I had no idea where the hell Bien Hoa was, but it was definitely Vietnam. (I looked at a Vietnam map when I got home and found out it was near Saigon.) It was hot. Until that moment, I didn't recall knowing anybody who had come back from there who wasn't injured or dead. But we were greeted by thousands of guys standing in line waiting to get on our plane to go home. They all seemed healthy and very happy to see us. They put us on buses and took us someplace, riding past civilian people walking ... and didn't even give us weapons. At night ... scary. It may have been Long Binh.

The next sunrise, Bob and I were bent, folded, spindled, and mutilated. Stand in line, fill out paperwork, get used to the heat. The most significant "fill out" was my DEROS date (estimated date to return Stateside). We referred to the States as "the world" because for the next 365, we weren't in it. I lied and considered the start of my tour to be March 7 (in Oakland).

A couple of days were spent filling sandbags and getting a mighty fine tan. Four days earlier I was in Syracuse in winter, cold and full of snow.

Bob and I made all the same lists and ended up on some sort of military plane (I think it was a C-130), headed to Pleiku. No frills, no flight attendants, beverages, or food. Just a mesh strap seat. About all I remember was the pilot telling us if a red light came on to "hang on tight." About then my "scared" index went over 10. Somewhere in that sifting and sorting, Bob and I separated. He went to 3/12, I went to 1/8 on 3/21. Confusion starts here, as I ended up in An Khe (we probably traveled by convoy), assigned to HHQ, 1/8, all medics, clerks, and cooks. Even though these were large installations, the VC gave us training on how to get into a bunker. Fast. Their training materials consisted of rockets and mortars.

SP-5 Ray Hubbard (right) filling sandbags at Dak To Base. Other soldier unknown.

I got some nice new jungle fatigues, shiny new boots (that would only have a hint of black in a few weeks), a rucksack, two canteens (that usually had hot Kool-Aid) and, I think, an M16. Then there was this mystery bag, my medical aid kit. Band-Aids, big and small; 15 morphines; and lots of tubes and bottles of stuff.

HHQ didn't really need me, so they "loaned" me to Delta Company. Delta was a "line" infantry company. These guys were "grunts," the aid station guys Jimmy Hendricks, Gary Dalegowski, and Vince. I think I met the med platoon leader, a lieutenant (Bartels). Nice guys. They taught me about the pills and bottles, morphine, and Band-Aids, things that my AIT kind of glazed over.

Anyhow, Delta Company was busy at the time with Operation Wayne Grey near Dak To, so I was just supposed to hang out. Arrangements were

SP-5 Ray Hubbard at Aid Station Dak To Base.

made to make two intermediate stops on my way to the ultimate assignment: 3rd Platoon, or 3rd Herd, of D Company. First stop was a large place called Mary Ann, or Mary Lou ... not sure which. Hell, I might have been to both, not sure. The VC reinforced our training, although infrequently, with rockets. I had to write down what Novahistine was used for, but I sure remembered how to get into a bunker. I was supposed to fly by helicopter out to meet the 3rd, but the copters were too full of resupply bullets and food, they didn't have room for me. The following day, March 21, I was told to get in a jeep with a lieutenant and one other "grunt." We got in on the end of a huge-ass convoy, headed to, presumably, the 3rd. Well, that convoy got blasted way up front. I remember seeing our tanks and APCs on a ridge overlooking the road, shooting and being shot at. My "holy crap meter" was in the red again. The convoy was turning around and going past us. Some Vietnamese were running past us as well, including a group of five or six carrying a guy in a blanket. The lieutenant said, "Doc, see what you can do for him. If you can't do anything in 60 seconds, get back in the jeep." Hell, I couldn't count the bullet holes the guy had in 60 seconds. My first time seeing bullet holes. During that brief time, I saw a truck with 3/12 markings on it as part of the retreat. So back to Mary Lou I went for another day. Was I headed for Blackhawk? Don't know. I sent a letter to Bob Hardison suggesting his unit was near mine and we should get together for a beer. I got that letter back from the Department of the Army stating "undeliverable," as he had been killed in action. Holy shit, we only just got here two weeks ago. I sent a condolence letter to his mom and received a reply telling me he had been killed in an ambush on March 27. Probably in that damn convoy. I learned Bob received a Distinguished Service Cross for his bravery that day. His mom's letter said he was initially listed as missing in action for several days, but only because it took two weeks to recover his body from a rice paddy. He was identified only by dental records. His family never got to see him again. His mom got a letter from him, after she was notified of his death, and he told her he was going out on his first patrol. Shit, he was only in-country two weeks. I actually have that notice from the Department of the Army, and Bob's mother's letter, which means I must have mailed them home. I can't imagine what my family thought, as I was a good little liar and never said I was in any danger in my letters.

About March 22, I headed by helicopter to an FB somewhere way out there. It took me 44 years and Frank Thomas to find out it was Firebase 20. That hill had two "mounds," one being a helipad, the other having grunts (*grunts = the guys who walk everywhere, with guns and stuff) and 105 artillery. The battalion aid doctor (Capt. Matt Howard) was supposed to "brief" me on all the meds I had and sort of give me a pep talk. I was on the helipad next to some C rations stacks, supposed to get on a helicopter headed for the 3rd, when the bad guys shot artillery at us. Artillery, you say. Yeah, artillery? Where did they get that shit? From Laos, or Cambodia, it doesn't matter which—we were that damn close (6,000 meters or six klicks is pretty freaking close). I ran like hell toward the other mound, hearing distant "thumps." Knowing crap was on its way, I sheltered on the opposite side of the saddle and listened to whistles of shells going over me and a few close hits. I ultimately found a bunker that was damp inside and about 10 feet deep. When it was over, the bastards hit the pile of C rats and one of the arty parapets. Some wounded and maybe dead, I got to see my first medevac, and spend a little time with Doc Howard. It's 45 years later, and I'm just now reading that all platoons of Delta Company were in and out of that Firebase 20, but I never knew it. And Doc Howard earned a Bronze Star that day.

The most common, most famous, was the Huey. They were the workhorse, moving my butt from place to place. Two pilots and two door gunners

SP-5 Ray Hubbard (right) waiting on a helicopter at Dak To Base. Other soldiers unknown.

with M60s allowed for eight guys inside. Three sat in each doorway with legs dangling out. No seat belts! Two guys on the inside. The pilots' heads were covered with helmets, but I often wondered about them. Were they just some 20-year-old kid with 10 weeks of "how to fly" training? I will say, they were good at it, and had balls of steel. Doors were usually removed. I had seen them equipped with mini-guns that could spray an immense number of bullets in seconds, subjecting the bad guys to lead poisoning. I had even seen them equipped with spray arms similar to a crop duster, spraying defoliant, later to be known as Agent Orange, subjecting everyone to a different kind of poisoning. But I can say, there weren't any trees or bushes within 100 yards of any road I walked down. They put red crosses on them and stretchers inside and it became a medevac (the most heroic guys in the war). They had a jungle penetrator, or a fold-down seat on a cable that they could drop down through heavy trees on a cable so they could "extract" wounded guys while the pilot kept the bird absolutely still. Up to three guys at a time. Of course, Hueys also ferried most of our supplies. The sound a Huey makes is very distinct and, to those who heard one, is unforgettable. Haunting, actually. I hope nobody ever complains about having a long drive to work.

Just a note about these helicopters: When we were told we were going to travel by helicopter, it sure sounded easier than walking. Except they called it a "combat assault." I'm thinking "assault" isn't a friendly word,

Dave Furlough, RTO, Dak To Base.

and to embellish it with "combat" sounds kind of scary. Wherever you are not being shot at, they are going to take you someplace where you will be. In a hurry. So, somebody says go sit in the doorway of that helicopter and you do it without thinking—that's the training, I suppose. So, of course, you duck because you mentally have to, the rotor is spinning at invisibility speed and pretty much over your head. But you have to. Now sitting in the doorway with all your shit, ya look around for something to hold on to. There is nothing there. The inside edge of the doorway, maybe. Or the guy next to you, and he has an equal amount of nothing. I mean, if you fall out, he's going with you. Just maybe you can brace yourself by putting your feet on the runner skid—but nope. Too far away. Then there is a lurch, and sort of liftoff... followed by very fast forward speed at an altitude of almost nothing. You can't see forward (thankfully), so a little prayer for the trees you last looked at around the LZ. Taking your mind off the impending "combat," you might look at the landscape below and, really, Vietnam is quite pretty. Practically, you consider the possibility of "combat" and think, "If I need to use my M16, I will need to use two hands, if only to get the safety off. Whatever chunk of metal I'm holding on to, I'm not letting go. And what if I need to reload?"

Cobra gunships were a one-man arsenal, miniguns delivering thousands of lead poison per minute and, I think, up to six rockets. I had the experience of being supported by these guys, and it's an awesome sight. They can just sit still and pinpoint the bad guys. This one instance, I heard a pilot on the radio say, "There are 'little people' 100 yards in front of you and I am going to expend a little Class 5 (bullets and shit)." I heard him on the radio but didn't actually see him until he let go of the stuff. He snuck up behind us and was directly over our head! God, I was in a great army.

There were also Loach helicopters. A small plastic bubble with a rotor. They were used for observation mostly, but some of the crazy pilots would play hide-and-seek with the gooks. The first guy would hover over the treetops with the intent of drawing fire. Once he did, the second guy would swoop in with miniguns firing until the barrels melted. Sounds like fun, eh?

Cranes and Chinooks were the workhorses. The "crane" could relocate a tank or damn near anything. The Chinook, or "shit hook," had interior cargo or personnel capacity and dual rotors, and I saw them used to relocate artillery pieces, huge harnesses full of artillery ammo, and 500-gallon rubber balloons with either water or gas. Ya just didn't want to be near them when they landed or took off as they made for one hell of a sand blaster, and my skin didn't care for it.

I finally got on a helicopter late in the day and flew to some hill occupied by just the 3rd Platoon. Met platoon leader Lt. Bob Ponzo and platoon Sgt. Gary Lysne.

SP-5 Ray Hubbard (center) building a command post in the bush. Other soldiers unknown.

"Welcome to the 3rd Herd ... when we work, we work hard, when we play, we play hard ... you have guard duty between eight and 10." This was no basic training exercise guard duty. Up to this point, I was in a reasonably "secure" environment, or so I thought. This was different. Real bad guys. "Trying to kill you" bad guys. No "Halt, who goes there" crap. These guys precede their approach with bullets of various sizes. And they don't halt. You have serious internal conversations with yourself how you are going to react, as you look into the bushes and trees, trying to see anything that moves, or sounds that aren't supposed to be there. But I was 20 years old, in great shape, and had a fully loaded M16. Safety off. And a bunch of guys to get me through this. So, my scared index is way above 10 again. My new radio call names were "Band-Aid," "5 niner," "Delta Oscar Charley," and even heard "Ben Casey" used once. The previous platoon medic had rotated out of country and a grunt was carrying his old aid bag, which he gladly turned over to me. I began writing names and passing out malaria pills first day. Initially it was simply quinine pills for falciparum malaria, but soon expanded to a weekly "horse tablet" to include vivax. It had become such an epidemic, the army required a urine sample from everyone to validate their taking it. They were reluctant as it gave them diarrhea. One guy who had taken it filled several cups, or they used a liquid that looked like urine: beer. No one got caught doing that. My casual enforcement attitude was if you want to get malaria, go ahead, and don't take it. The night watch would wake me first every day and I would personally drop a daily pill in each guy's mouth when I woke them. While in Dak To, these guys got into some bad water, as dysentery ran rampant, or as I recorded in my log, "shits."

It didn't take too long to take for granted the distant thumps of artillery mortars and sometimes small arms fire. Nighttime in the bush made the days look good. It was always there. As long as it didn't involve you, you just shrugged it off. Did I mention, it was always there?

On April 6, Easter Sunday, we cleared an area where a Loach helicopter could land, and soon our battalion chaplain (Don Little) did just that. And, using a log for an altar, gave us an Easter service. Quite impressive. We also got mail, a hot meal (beef, potatoes, corn and bread, milk), and S/P boxes with candy and cigarettes. In a letter to my dad, I referred to Lieutenant Ponzo losing his compass and getting us lost. Platoon strength was 27. Per a letter home, we arrived at Blackhawk April 14, and on to An Khe on the 18th.

April 18, we had been in An Khe (Camp Radcliff) for four days. At either of these places, we got hot meals and showers, making you realize things you used to take for granted. We went walking for a couple of days (not covered in AIT), introducing me to hills and jungle and rice paddies. Considering my cement head city background, I was noting the Vietnamese "workforce" in the rice paddies to be mostly women (in pajamas and a cone-shaped straw hats). Adult males were probably in the army. And standing beside the rice paddy would be water buffalo, monsters that cultivated, harvested, and fertilized the rice. Seemingly docile unless provoked, they would just look at you as you passed. I was warned never to shoot at one, as all an M16 would do is piss it off, and there is nothing worse than a pissed-off water buffalo. Some areas involved jungle that had been previously "arc lighted" (significant 1,000-pound bomb runs with a B52). I suppose we were expected to recover enemy bodies or something, but what we found was impenetrable mass of twisted trees and jungle. Lysne and Ponzo told me I didn't need to know anything, just walk behind the guy with the radio. I did both for the remainder of the year. Dave Furlough was one RTO, Ernie Roland was another, I'm not sure which one I followed. These

SP-5 Ray Hubbard (top), Lysne, and Harris at Dak To Base.

guys knew what it was all about, and I suppose they expected me to know my medic stuff. Little did they know, most of what I needed to know I got from OJT with them. These guys had just been in some encounters near Dak To, so we were headed for a stand-down. Blackhawk, I believe. (Confirmed in letter to Dad—April 17 we were in Blackhawk, came from Khontoum, on our way to An Khe.) Fresh clothes, hot food, and showers. If it wasn't Blackhawk, it was An Khe, maybe both. At some point, we were in the huge base of An Khe (Camp Radcliff or McNerny, per John Nolan). Shortly thereafter, the entire company took a walk, a long walk down a road (QL 19, I'm told by Sgt. Ted Bahle, about 30 years later). Soon, a convoy showed up, with tons of stuff, including 105 mm artillery and a bulldozer. It took about three days to "clear" that hill with the bulldozer. All the while, we went on either short sweeps (sweep = a walkabout, sometimes just woods, sometimes roads and villages) of six or 10 klicks of the area or road guard duty. This was to become Firebase Denise. We spent days policing bulldozer leftovers (chunks of trees, brush), either burning it or preserving larger logs to use as cover or bunkers. I came upon a "chunk" of log that wasn't log—it was a snake, about three feet long, eight inches diameter. We found three chunks altogether, never finding the head, but it was no doubt a python that had been sleeping with us on that hill for three days (NOT covered in AIT). If someone ever tells me they had a bad night's sleep, I will probably just roll my eyes. When not walking or policing, we filled sandbags for bunkers. Line bunkers first. Lots of sandbags. (Another AIT omission.) After the first 5,000 or so sandbags, ya sort of get used to it. We had a hole about two feet deep, with sandbag walls begun, as the start of the platoon command post bunker. We went on one of our daily walks, and I was introduced to another form of Vietnamese weather: rain. As serious as the heat was, the rain is just as serious. Upon return to Denise, we found that the entire hill drained right through my "hooch."

We had us a swimming pool! We had to tear it apart, drain it, and start over, only to have one of the finest bunkers in Vietnam. Slept five. Ammo crate table. Ammo crate window shutters and door, and a wood diversion in front of the door to keep water from running in. The TOC (tactical operation command) bunker had generated electric lighting and Gary demonstrated Army "bartering," and we found ourselves with a wire from that generator and a light for our bunker. We thought it was uptown, but really, it was pretty dumb.

May 22, Ponzo left for a job in the rear. I have learned in recent years he was put in charge of the Kit Carson Scout program, enemy soldiers who surrendered and went to work for us as point men and informants and interpreters. The two we had assigned to us weren't much help. I believe we stayed on "Denise" a couple of months doing daily patrols around the area, and every few days walking to Radcliff in An Khe to establish road security for convoys of trucks to come to Denise. There were engineers assigned to us, and they would walk in front of us with a metal detector, looking for land mines. They walked so fast, you really wondered about their effectiveness. I suspect the 25 guys walking behind them were more effective, but we never saw one. Sitting on the side of that road, I was introduced to a new phenomenon. Vietnamese locals would stop and "sell" or barter anything—soda, cigs, drugs, and even their daughters. This was a very uneasy situation, as you never knew if they were friendly or Vietcong, going to blow you away. I never got used to trusting anyone with slanted eyes. If they didn't have what you wanted, they would hop on a motorcycle and run to town and get it. Military currency (MPC) or Vietnamese piasters were used. The slang term "Souvenir me a _____" came into being, usually a cigarette. *Dinky dau* meant sick in the head or crazy, number

SP-5 Ray Hubbard using a makeshift shower.

10 was bad, number one was good. The "ladies" (boom-boom girls) proclaimed "me number one meat, no sick dick." The French influence 20 years earlier gave us *beaucoup dinky dau* (very crazy). *Di di mau* meant "get out quickly."

When not on patrols, I was informed it was the medic's duty to oversee field sanitation. This totally was not covered in AIT. "Piss tubes" were easy ... drill some holes in an artillery canister, put it in a hole with drainage rocks, put a sandbag "filter" over the opening, and stick it in the ground. The "shitter" was another story, but I came up with a sandbag crate turned on end, the hinged lid becoming the door, and a few other modifications for a half steel drum underneath, and a toilet seat, provided by base camp. The engineers would take a 55-gallon drum, empty, of course, wrap it with "det cord"—C4 plastic explosive shaped like a rope—and poof, "half barrels." The half barrels were rotated daily, and diesel fuel put on the waste, and burned—with stirring. Not a lot of fun. But Sergeant Lysne informed me I was only "in charge" of sanitation, not necessarily having to do it. Hence, on occasion, he would send me a couple of guys needing a punishment, and they got to do the dirty work. As for showers, I took the easy way out: a couple of two-by-fours stuck in the ground, a cross member that held the canvas "shower" bag over your head. (I believe they were called a "Lister" bag.) Five gallons of "room temp" water, I believe. (No frills, and no modesty.) The showerhead fixture opened and closed, so soaping up and rinsing off was the extent of the five gallons. Water could be warmed in two ways: by leaving a five-gallon metal canister of water sitting in the sun all day (Did I mention the average daily temp was around 100 or more?) or the ever-popular C4 (plastic explosive) ignited underneath it. At a later date, we also ignited leftover pellet charges from 155 artillery to rapidly heat water or C rations.

Approximately June 2, the 3rd Herd was split up due to low head count. SFC Anderson became platoon leader, Lysne platoon sergeant, and I was one of two medics in the new 2nd Platoon. The other guy was a six-day

SP-5 Ray Hubbard aiding a Vietnamese boy in a nearby village.

wonder, an ordinary infantry guy trained in six days by the battalion aid surgeon in medical basics.

At some point on Denise, I was taught to do MEDCAPs (Medical Civil Action Plan). It was about this time our president, LBJ, decided we could win the war not by bombing the place but by winning the hearts and minds of the local people. Essentially, M (the town doctor) would trot off to a village and treat whoever was left there, usually old women and kids. Healthy males were off in the army ARVN or the Vietcong (sometimes both). Security was provided by my platoon or at least a squad (seven grunts, with guns) or two. Medical Civil Action Plan was defined as treating any civilian … in any manner. I learned that *dau dau* meant headache, *dau boom* meant stomachache, *dau loung* meant backache. *Hot/cold* meant fever. I was a "boxie," Vietnamese for doctor. Cuts got Band-Aids, mama-san got soap, the village chief got chewing tobacco, and kids got candy courtesy of S/P packs that supplemented our rations of C rations. Upon returning to the firebase, I was presented with a form to fill out by the company medic describing my day. I was told to make it add up to 100, but hell, I didn't even see 100 people all day. (This came to be known many years later as Westmoreland math.) But, one Band-Aid counted, one candy bar, a drop of mercurochrome, one aspirin. Exaggeration went a long way on that form. My guess is about 300 percent. Westmoreland approved! There were 10 villages surrounding Denise. I usually saw one a day. These MEDCAPs were incorporated into the daily "sweeps" we were making anyway. The exaggerations continued almost daily.

My recollection was that we worked from Denise in May, June, and July.

Letters home indicate we had been on Denise 51 days on 12 June. Until it was named, I called it FB WIA, "where I'm at." Jungle rot was a frequent malady, an occasional leech, and diarrhea. Guys that had the fortune of visiting town, or the roadside boom-boom girl, sometimes got the clap. They would be sent to base camp, penicillin in the ass (and ridden around camp in a jeep with seat cushions removed, if Captain Caldwell had his way). I recall being on guard duty at night looking toward Camp Radcliff watching helicopter gunships doing perimeter security with amazing streams of red tracers swirling down from the sky.

Pot was readily available and seemingly overlooked by those in charge. Peer pressure brought about the pot squad. On any established or temporary night location, a three-man LP, or listening post, would be sent about 100 yards from the perimeter and take turns staying awake all night. If the pot smoker fell asleep, they all were in jeopardy the rest of the night. Squad size missions had the same setup. So, the dopes were all put together and the feeling was, if they fell asleep, it didn't jeopardize

SP-5 Ray Hubbard holding a clean pair and wearing a dirty pair of fatigues.

anyone else. Sergeant Lysne frequently confiscated pot and tossed it into the wind. I wonder if any seeds sprouted. Casual mama-sans also made available opium drops that would be rubbed on a cigarette and inhaled that way. It is said that it takes all kinds in the army, and we had our share of idiots. My job on guard at night was to call all LP posts and ask for a "sit rep," or situation report. If there was no reply, they were asleep, and a flare was fired in their direction to roust them. Actually, I'm told one LP was actually tripped over by a couple of VC, but I don't remember it directly.

Other significant events were the changing of company commander from Capt. Ted Yamashita to Capt. Archibald Caldwell (approximately April). Unfortunately, I was so busy micromanaging my platoon sick call, field sanitation, and MEDCAPs, I have no recollection of Ted. Also, approximately May 16, the 4th Platoon (led by Lt. John Nolan) was hit on one of their daily sweeps. Point man Joe Fowler was killed. We watched and listened to it from Denise, as it wasn't far off. Captain Caldwell assembled a platoon and went to assist. Third and one other platoon remained on

Denise as FB security. I remember watching smoke rise from the area and was told F14 jets were dropping napalm near the action.

The initial issue of two quarts of water was insufficient, and I decided to never run out again. I scavenged another seven. I also "acquired" a "special forces" aid bag, which was much larger, and, fixed to the top of my ruck, made me top-heavy and unable to stand by myself. Walking was okay, just getting up was a bitch. I also decided never to be hungry again, so I also "scavenged" any throwaway date puddings from platoon C rations. It was a dense little bread-like thing that could fill you up all day. Guys hated them and frequently "86'd" (destroyed) them. Optionally, you could "backhaul" (send in for repair) something. Dx referred to clean fatigues, which we got every three days maybe. There was a pile of shirts, pants, and socks. You walked past and picked one of each. SIZE DIDN'T MATTER. There was no underwear—we were all commandos. I was also able to order prenatal vitamins, another secret to keep from going hungry. I dispersed them freely.

Mail was a huge priority, a huge morale factor. I started getting mine very early on. Mostly from my dad and sister and girlfriend, Sharon. Not just letters, but an occasional package of goodies. I requested anyone sending a letter to put a pack of presweetened Kool-Aid in the envelope. That was to remove the taste of the pills we had to put in drinking water. We used one to four pills, depending on the source and "color" of the water. "Four-pill water" was pretty nasty, and it was always hot.

The phrase "Ya can't get them unless ya send them" held true, so I wrote Dad, sister, and girlfriend as often as I could. No postage required, we simply wrote "free" where the stamp would go, and just to ensure we got "air mail" priority, we wrote "fly it," as well. There wasn't much to say, and I sure didn't tell them any of the bad stuff, so I wrote to everyone I could think of that I had an address for and got a pretty good response.

Base camp mail was very good, but when we were remote, that red mailbag was on every helicopter we had resupplying us. None of the choppers had doors, so, regardless of what else was on board, you could see that red mailbag for miles. It felt good.

> HOME, 8 July: We had left Denise and spent four days above Mang Yang Pass (we were on Mang Yang July 4.; thankfully no fireworks). On that date we went to LZ Schueller, the place with the tankers (LZ = landing zone, no artillery, but this particular one had tanks). We only stayed a couple of days but were told it was a long-term assignment. We were resupplied with everything, including beer and soda, but they immediately ordered to send out all squads on "missions." That left the platoon CP (lieutenant, sergeant, two RTOs, and the medic). So, we drank beer and played cards in a lovely bunker. It rained, and the bunker leaked. A tanker guy came in and attempted to position a cot in any place it wouldn't get dripped on and failed. I sure didn't feel sorry for a guy who had a cot to sleep on. He left and went back to sleep in

his tank. I awoke next morning alone, lying across three air mattresses, floating in about a foot of water, drunk as a skunk.

I'm sure that in August, we established a new FB down the road from Denise, away from An Khe, called FB Amelia, named after the battalion commander's wife. HOME: We built Amelia on 23 July. There was a Colonel Buckner, battalion commander, but I'm not sure if he was in charge at that time. Whoever was commander was nicknamed "Bullet," as our battalion was named "Bullets."

Again, a bulldozer was sent out to dig holes for 1/69th mechanized armor 155 howitzers. For the first few pre-bunker days, I slept on my air mattress about 20 yards behind one of them. About sundown, the first of 150 volleys from all five 155s went off, lasting through the night. I remember my air mattress came off the ground with each one. And loud ... very, very loud. Forty-plus years later, I have severe tinnitus and hearing loss. Bunker building, field sanitation, and medic "stuff" prevailed, and I was informed the 1/69th had no medics, so I was "it" for them as well. Westmoreland math became obvious when a division newspaper reported that on a specific MEDCAP day, the 1st/69th teamed with 1st/8th to treat 3,000 people. Knowing our company was the only one sitting on a firebase doing MEDCAPs, and that I was the medic for the 1st/69th, I'm guessing that

SP-5 Ray Hubbard in a bulldozer with a mechanized 155 mm howitzer.

number of 100 inflated at the company level, then again at the battalion level, brigade, and so on. Early on, we received a new guy, PFC Campbell. We periodically got FNGs (f'ing new guys). He reenlisted for a second tour, so he was "experienced." Ha! His first day filling sandbags, he removed his shirt and got a fire-red sunburn for which he consulted Captain Caldwell (the company commander, not his medic—me). Captain told me, "You had better do whatever you can for him because if he is unable to work tomorrow, we would court-martial him." I mopped him down with calamine lotion and hoped for the best. It worked. "Soup," as he became known, loved an M79 grenade launcher and became the maker of "foo gas" (some sort of concoction with gasoline, diesel fuel, and other stuff, stirred up in a 55-gallon drum with a boat paddle). I have heard it referred to as "homemade napalm." Sergeant Lysne told him to go stir the concoction together. When he was noticed missing that evening, he was found by the

Nothing left of Firebase Amelia.

perimeter ... still stirring. Lysne asked him why he didn't come in, and he responded, "You didn't tell me to stop." When ignited with a blasting cap, it was a devastating defensive weapon. There were several placed around Amelia. This period was more sweep.

MEDCAPs, and filling sandbags. About a month later, we destroyed everything we didn't put on our backs, and went walking again. During our stay on Amelia, we had a visit from George Gobel, TV celebrity. His son was a 4th aviation pilot and instead of his son returning home, "Lonesome George" came to get him ... and visited troops in the field. Upon arrival, his helicopters were sent on another mission and Captain Caldwell told him until they got back, we could only offer him a chair and some beer. He said he didn't need the chair, but don't run out of beer. He stood there and did about an hour of stand-up jokes, then posed for pictures with anyone that wanted to. Someone forgot to disarm a foo gas at the helipad, and when George and his entourage left, Captain Caldwell found it and got a bit mad. He wanted to know who was responsible for him having to explain how we turned George Gobel into a crispy critter (a helicopter discharges static electricity and could have fired off the blasting cap beneath the foo gas but didn't in this case).

According to labels on my pictures, we went to an FB named Schueler about September, but I remember almost nothing about it, except we didn't build it, we just occupied it.

Sometime in this period we also built and/or occupied FB Julia. A short period later, we returned to Denise, which was in the hands of C Company. I was jealous they had created a poncho privacy curtain around the showers with ponchos and metal or wood posts. It was here on September 1, according to letters home, Jim Wazniak sat at a table, cleaning his M60 after cleaning his .45.

Because of its rarity, Sgt. Joe Scala sat across from Jim and "played" with the .45, accidentally shooting Wazniak through the chest, then the web of the hand of one of our RTOs (Stevens). The entire company was present as I remember four medics attending to the classic sucking chest wound. I diverted to Stevens's hand. It seemed like an hour before medevac arrived, taking them to 4th Med (hospital). With him being charged with involuntary manslaughter, we took turns guarding Scala in the command bunker till next day. Chaplain Little came next morning to tell us we did a good job on Wazniak; he was alive when he got to 4th Med. They worked on him for four hours but lost him in the end. Chaplain Little also announced his impending rotation "back to 'the world.'" At some time during the Denise revisit, we had "donut dollies" and Johnny Grant (Armed Forces Radio personality; he was known as the poor man's Bob Hope as he would come to Vietnam with as many girls as he could muster and bring them to forward areas—he didn't wait for once a year at Christmas)—and bring a morale boost in the form of Miss California, Miss Indiana, and Donna de Varona, a '64 US Olympic swimmer.

July '69

Among some of the periodic walks in the woods, we got to relocate via helicopter. Many CAs (combat assaults), not sure when they occurred. I should have received an Air Medal for flying more than six combat assaults, but never did. Remember, I was in HHQ Company technically, and they had no idea what I was doing. I never protested but Lysne said everybody in our platoon got one. Oh well, that and a dime will get you a cup of coffee, back in "the world." One "eventful CA," we were waiting in an area, and our boy "Soup" accidentally skipped a grenade round through the middle of us standing there. The round didn't go off, but Captain Caldwell sure did. We flew to a hillside that was deemed a "hot" LZ (hot in this case means they be shootin', you need to be duckin' and dodging), therefore they weren't going to land but come close—and it was up to us

Lloyd Burel, M-60 machine gunner, at Firebase Schueffer.

to jump. They were partly right; it wasn't a hot LZ. But five-foot-high tree stumps prevented any landing, so jumping was from 10 feet or so ... with a full rucksack ... and aid bag and nine quarts of water. If I am right, we proceeded to the foot of Mang Yang Pass. We were promptly loaded up with full meals, ammo, and mail and told to climb the mountain overlooking the pass. I have to thank my dad for the tons of cyclamate presweetened Kool-Aid and the Jolly Time popcorn in that mail drop. And another 10 pounds of cookies and brownies from sister. The prospect of hauling that popcorn up that mountain wasn't good, so I dumped it in a campfire. The plan changed. So, they decided to fly us up to the top and Greg West snatched my popcorn and damn if he didn't pop it that night on the mountaintop. Thinking back, flying up that "hill" was easier than climbing it, but, because of the height, the air sort of thins out, and listening to the Huey rotor struggling to get us up, my holy crap meter was topped out again. About this time, Lt. Steven North (butter bar, second lieutenant) was our platoon leader. Lysne had gone on R&R to Hawaii with his wife. That mountaintop was soaking wet, as clouds covered it each morning. Leeches galore. We couldn't guard the road below; we couldn't see it! We walked off it two or three days later.

> HOME, 18 Aug 69: I referred to the new platoon leader as an idiot because when we did a MEDCAP he asked everyone if they were VC. Confirmed by Lysne, it was a Lieutenant Haven, we nicknamed him Hawkeye. He would walk down a road with his M16 in firing position looking through the sights the whole way. He only lasted a couple of weeks as he got wounded on some patrol.

There was a snake encounter sometime. We walked in the woods and the RTO (Ernie Roland) pulled his antenna down and duck-walked under an arch formed by the brush. I half bent over and started through, when he spun around and said, "Don't move." I looked in his direction and was face-to-face with a bamboo viper lying in the bush at eye level. Nicknamed "a step and a half" as their poison allowed you to get that far after being bitten. It was a pretty green snake but some guy with a machete removed him from my path. Per letter home, 18 October, we occupied FB Armageddon. It had vehicle remnants of the French occupying it many years earlier.

Per letter home, we were on FB Patricia sometime in October '69. My pictures indicate a Firebase Knaak that I had no recollection of until discussion with Glenn Sattler and reviewing photo labels.

On another occasion, 3rd Platoon was out walking the jungle and settled in a temporary night location on a hillside. In the morning, the squad leader, Sgt. Rick Kreuger, took three men down ahead of the remaining platoon, to a small river. He saw footprints and followed them, only to be shot in the arm by a single VC. We heard no return fire, and I was rushed to the site. Rick was lying on his back, and from elbow to shoulder,

(Fom left) Miss California, Miss Indiana, and Donna de Varona, 1964 U.S. Olympic swimmer, visiting troops in Vietnam.

were a few pieces of meat. My AIT training or my instinct kicked in and I wrapped it in a large bandage, put the arm in a cravat, and laid it on his chest. I gave him morphine and began filling out a medical incident card. Well, that card wanted to know name, rank, serial number, where it happened, what happened, and 300 other questions I couldn't answer. I diverted to assembling a serum albumin (a blood volume expander used in acute blood loss). I didn't have time to complete it. While I was busy, a call was made to medevac and denied as we hadn't "secured" the area, but some chaplain happened to be in the area in a three-man Loach helicopter and said he would come for him. It landed on some rocks in the river, and Rick was pushed into the back seat beside that chaplain. Because I hadn't indicated on the med tag that I had given morphine, I stood on the chopper's skid screaming at the chaplain, "Tell them he has had morphine," several times. It seemed like that chaplain didn't want to see any blood and he looked straight ahead until he finally turned toward me and nodded acknowledgment. When I turned to get off the runner, we were in flight! I had to jump into the damn river about 20 feet. Well, maybe only 10, but it was scary. About one year later, while I was stationed at Fort Lewis, Washington, I ran into a medic who said his brother-in-law was in my unit in Vietnam, and was shot, sent home. Guess who? Rick Kreuger. I immediately phoned him in Chesterton, Indiana, and after catching him up on the outcomes of his buddies, he announced he had one more surgery on his arm pending, which would give him 90 percent use of it. For once, I felt like I did something right, or at least had a part in it. On the following day, we were sitting next to that same river hearing a dog barking from across it. Shortly, a sniper took a shot at our perimeter and the lucky shot got a guy (forgot his name) in the leg. It was "book stuff" and I took care of business, and medevac showed up this time. A second minor injury occurred from that incident, I don't remember who or what. Did I fill out a med tag? Don't know. To this day, I am haunted and wonder about every bandage I put on: Did I do it right? Was it tight enough? It just seems like everything was never enough.

If I remember right, all of this was during a memorable 33-day "hike." It seemed like we got wet every day. If it didn't rain, we did a river crossing. Every day. Thirty-three days stand out because, at the end, we pushed for a location that was amenable for the Army to send us a pay officer, and it was either the fifth or the eighth of October. Shopping in the jungle wasn't in the cards, but the Army was concerned for us not having any money. The end of this hike is a bit fuzzy, but we went up a mountain—all day—with a firebase at the top of it. When we got there, it was the wrong mountain. So, we went back down, and up another one. It was the wrong one too. We rendezvoused with other D Company elements. At one point we were supposed to be walking along a ridgeline and the point kept drifting off the side. From the rear, Sergeant Lysne called and pointed it out, and we corrected. (Remember, I was always behind the RTO.) About the fourth time of drifting, I heard, "Can't anybody up there read a damn compass?" On the third attempt to find our "mountain," it rained. It was an all-day "UP." And into the night. Way into the night. It was so dark, we literally were holding on to the rifle of the man in front of us. Lots of rain, lots of mud. Boots on the trail made a rut slot on the side of that hill. Around midnight, the point platoon reached the top, and guess what? No firebase ... wrong mountain! A call was put out for artillery flares to shoot up so we could fix our position. At least for guys who had maps, compasses, and knew that kind of stuff. When word came back we would stay put till daybreak, I was wet, tired, miserable, and pissed. Everything I owned was soaked, so no point in opening up a bedroll (poncho + nylon poncho liner + air mattress). Preferring not to slide down into the boot-made mud rut, or off the mountain entirely, I positioned a tiny tree between my legs, folded my arms in disgust, and would simply wait out morning. I didn't even remove my pack. As it turned out, I slid off that tree and woke up lying in that mud trail with a poncho over me. How the poncho got there, I don't know. But, seeing what appeared to be a discarded poncho, Gary Lysne picked it up and found me mired beneath it. I probably passed out malaria pills before we went down the hill and up a new one where we finally found our goal. A pay officer flew out to pay us. What I remember about that firebase was C Company occupied it and had been overrun by NVA a couple of days before we got there. They were regular NVA and "sappers." These sneaky little sapper guys would strip down to a loin cloth, strap a couple of satchel charges over their shoulder, and crawl right into your perimeter in a matter of seconds, avoiding trip flares, razor wire, claymore mines, and grenade trip traps. Once inside, they would wreak havoc slitting throats

Steve North (left) and Ernie Roland in the bush.

and tossing satchel charges into bunkers of sleeping guys. It happened very fast. It wasn't a suicide mission, as they also usually got away. Sleeping that night was especially unnerving, the thought of NVA surrounding us. I slept with my boots on that night as my fear index was a 20 on a scale of 1 to 10. We walked away the next day with pay in our pockets, but very alert of our surroundings. I think our mission was to find and engage the NVA, but we didn't encounter them. Scary. A letter home indicates it was LZ Larry, and because I was HHQ Company, I had my own pay officer. Well, me and three other medics and officers.

Leading up to October 29, we were walking through the woods, in stealth mode, and the company was going down a hill toward a river. Stealth mode meant no resupply copters would be coming to us and giving away our presence. I already had one man with malaria and was refused a medevac. A man sprained an ankle on the hill, and he also was refused. Third Platoon was on the approach hill and other platoons on the other side of a pond-like area of the river. From out of nowhere, a North Vietnamese came out of the water to *chu hoi* (surrender). Initial indication was he was an NVA doctor, serving a covert hospital nearby. Soon after, we had a helicopter come with interpreters. That evening, Captain Caldwell tied a rope around the man's waist, gave him a flashlight, and made him show us where it was. I think 2nd Platoon (Lt. Bruce Simmons and Glenn Sattler) went with them. They had negative results. The doctor was flown back to Pleiku and upon further interrogation turned out to be an NVA general, as reported by the 4th Division newspaper. A rumor I heard was if you take two NVA or VC on a helicopter ride and push one of them out, the second one will tell you everything. Another stealth mission incident involved a man with severe abdominal pain that I couldn't relieve. He literally crawled to Captain Steedley (D Company command changed from Captain Caldwell to Capt. Homer Steedley) and begged for help. I consulted with the battalion doctor (Abijean) by radio, and his advice failed as well. Medevac refused to come to an unsecure area at night. Captain Steedley got on the radio with them and told them he refused to be responsible for the outcome of this man's ailment; they came an hour later without incident. Turned out, it was a kidney stone I could have never diagnosed or treated.

Another incident involved being in an area of no "friendlies" and we came upon an obvious grass hooch filled with supplies and housing some chickens and a pig. We burned the hooch, and shot the pig, about 1,000 times. That evening we set up near a stream and in the middle of the night, a guard set off a claymore mine due to an approaching noise. All fire was directed toward the outside of our perimeter until we could determine direction of the incoming fire. There was none. Investigation revealed that

SP-5 Ray Hubbard at Firebase Knaak.

a noisy pig had started up a trail toward us. The next morning, someone reported to Sergeant Lysne that one of the guys "freaked" and his "directional fire" went everywhere, and this particular reportee had two bullet holes in a gas mask he had been using as his pillow. I believe the man was Tom Archer, and he was to be watched. The following night we had taken a position along a trail, and Archer was on guard and began shooting for no apparent reason. Again, no incoming fire. It was determined to be falling leaves that startled him.

In an October 4, 1969, letter home, I described humping several days into LZ Larry.

Approximately October '69, we had a couple of interim COs between Caldwell and Steedley. Lt. Kent Goolsby was the second. The first guy was there approximately a week and was shot while on a patrol. I never met the guy—hell, I never even saw him. So, while out on a patrol, our boy "Soup" (who loved to suck up) sits down next to him, lifts his pants leg, and asks him, "I wonder what this is." His ankles and lower leg were covered in jungle rot. It seems "Soup" never took his boots off. Well, Goolsby jumped all over me and told me to check every man's feet every day. Yeah, right! Well 45 years later at a reunion in Townsend, Tennessee, there's this guy at a table saying that same story ... yup, Lieutenant Goolsby. I turned to the guys I was with and said, "Holy crap, he's talking about me! Small world, eh?" Goolsby was there only a couple of weeks, I didn't even remember his name.

Another event: After Mang Yang Pass, on October 29, we were walking toward An Khe (Camp Radcliff), along QL19 in late afternoon when VC threw a bunch of B40 rockets and mortars at us from an adjoining hill. This hill... We were on the opposite side of the same hill where Joe Fowler was killed in May. While we were on FB Denise, we sent out many platoon-size patrols on *that* same hill. (Confirmed by Gary Lysne and by Pat Calhoun some 40-plus years later.) I was told we saw evidence of artillery been moved through there (tire tracks).

An entire company out in the open, including a weapons platoon (mortars) trying to eat a C ration dinner. All of the incoming either went over our heads or bounced through our perimeter, the only casualties being opened C rations. We were totally exposed with only a few piles of rocks for cover. Our initial response was mortar return fire at puffs of smoke from the adjacent hill. By miraculous coincidence, a quad four (four .50-cal machine guns mounted on 55-gallon barrels, welded to the bed of a deuce and a half) happened down the road and stopped to assist.

About the "gun truck." This was no Pentagon-issued vehicle. Transport guys wanted protection on convoys anywhere they went, so, they stole armor plates, guns and made their own security. The NVA had issued bounties, and in my current reading, only one came back to the US and is in the Smithsonian. There are a few replicas floating around. At a reunion event, I saw "Wild Thing" magnificently recreated by the original crew. This one backed off the road facing the hill and started pouring bullets all over it. Delightful, except for the part of backing into a small gulley, causing the gunners to jerk, lift up the guns, then point them down and spray bullets right through our perimeter. Fortunately, no incidents. The follow-up consisted of artillery from Radcliff, small, fixed-wing aircraft dropping smoke markers, and then helicopter gunships. Lastly, F-14 jets poured bouncing Bettys and white phosphorus (also known as Willie Peter or Wilson Pickett) on the hill. That should do it. We slept right there on the roadside that night, and in the morning we were going up there to police up dead bodies. First Platoon took lead (I think 17 or 21 strong), followed by the company CP (a radio guy, 1st Sergeant Madden, Doc Keyes, and Capt. Homer Steedly). I came along in our platoon CP (myself, Lieutenant North, and an RTO) after our platoon point squad. About the time the trail took a dogleg right, all hell broke loose. I lay on the trail cuddled up next to a log. When I lifted my head to hear where shots were coming from, I thought I was on the wrong side of the log. So, I leapfrogged over it … two or three times. Hearing cries for "medic" coming from 1st Platoon, I lifted my head only to see 1st Sergeant Madden waving a finger at me, pointing me to move toward the calls. I knew it was my time. There was a very brief thought of what to do, when all of a sudden that "F it" attitude took over. I can't explain, ya just do it. I'm not sure why I took this job. If an enemy bullet trajectory hits a man, why would I have got to that place? It was the medic's job. I half remember thinking, "This is it. Is this how it's all going to end?" But there were too many other things to think about, so you don't. You just do it. I swear I heard Lieutenant North tell the remainder of the 3rd to retreat, separating us. Doc Keyes (who was 10 days from DEROS) and I moved forward, tending to one man at a time, leapfrogging past one another. I would drag a wounded guy back to the area where Captain Steedley was and tell him we had nobody shooting back at the bad guys, we need firepower up there. The whole 1st Platoon was "down." I could hear the crackle of bamboo breaking over my head from enemy gunfire. Dragging the next guy back to the CP, I requested firepower up front and was told, "You have five minutes, gunships are on the way." Holy crap,

(From left) SP-5 Ray Hubbard, Pete Harris, and Rich Kreager at Dak To.

I wanted to be gone when *that* happened!! About then, an M60 gunner and mate from 3rd Platoon came past me and began to set up. My thought was this is a good thing. If the gun hadn't malfunctioned, it would have been. They packed up their crap and returned back toward the CP. I thought "no problem," where's the rest of my guys?? But nothing. Keyes and I both left a man who had an obvious spinal wound. I barely knew him, but knew he was a nice guy. Possibly 1st Platoon leader? He got bandages.

    I remember making sure he had his M16 handy, and I just told him, "Don't shoot me or Keyes." He was comfortable, so we moved forward again, all the while thinking how in the hell we were going to move him. My next encounter with Captain Steedley, I was told, "You have five minutes, jets are on the way." (About 25 years later, I spoke to him and recounted those warnings and he said he was bluffing and only trying to hurry my ass up so we could get the hell out of there.) And then it happened. From way back, here comes Sgt. Ted Bahle (a 3rd Platoon squad leader) … alone … walking upright along the side of the trail, spraying the shit out of everything from the ground to the tops of trees. Awesome! The 3rd Herd was back up with us, and I felt a little better. Keyes and I got to the rest of the men, including the 1st Platoon medic (Clayton), whom I casually knew. He had the most bullet holes. We were told by the chaplain (the following day) that the medic "made it," which implied the others should have also. They're not on the Wall. Four men were dead, including a guy who was decapitated by a bullet entering his helmet and making a circle around, opening his skull like a can opener. When the smoke cleared, the 3rd Platoon appeared and carried back the dead and escorted seven walking wounded. I personally picked up every rifle, pistol belt, and any other crap lying along the trail. I must have looked like John Wayne/Rambo/Audie Murphy all in one. Back at the Steedley position, they were prepping to use a jungle penetrator on a medevac to pick up the wounded. The three worst went first. As the chopper hovered, bringing them up, through triple-canopy jungle, the bad guys shot at it as if it was a sitting duck. A copilot and a medic aboard were hit, but they stayed still hovering until our guys were on board. Gotta love 'em. I gathered faith that if I was wounded, I would be in good hands. The walking wounded walked (including Carl Locklear, Jim Norris, Billy Whitlow, Steve Marsolik, Robert Oliver, and Little Jack) and the dead were carried. Sgt. Gary Lysne had the duty of carrying the decapitated guy. We went through some nasty brush going down that hill, myself behind Doc Keyes. I noticed he had his holstered .45 cocked, which implied a round in the chamber, and asked him if the safety was on. When he looked and found it wasn't, he looked at me and turned absolutely white. Quite a color change for a Cajun guy. I remember telling him this wasn't a good time to accidentally shoot his leg off. Halfway down, we met a Huey, who took the dead bodies off our hands (Tom Clark, James Herrin, Perry Hopkins, and Wes Vermeesch), as well as most of the gear I was hauling and the walking wounded. Tom Archer sat down at this point, wet his pants, and cried. I gave him two Benadryl sedatives and he also was put on that chopper. I heard later that he was reassigned to the 4th Division newspaper as an artist. He was no longer a liability to us. We got back to the road and watched the fireworks of everything Steedley promised, artillery, gunships, and jets. We headed to Camp Radcliff; I think by truck. After a hot meal, we had a formation and the battalion commander addressed us with "we got our asses kicked and we are going right straight back there." We got a hot meal, mail, and a helicopter ride to the hill directly across the road from the previous hill. The following day we watched C Company go up that hill, uneventfully and not finding the 11 bodies of VC that the gunships said they got. My mail included a letter from Sharon, my back-home girlfriend, with an ultimatum: "Marry me when you come home, or else." It was a bad day to give me an ultimatum, so I fired back a reply that wasn't conducive to a long-term relationship. I knew that was a dead-end relationship because I was "busy" trying not to get killed for another six months, then I had another 18 months in the Army being sent to "who knows where," and I still wanted two more years of college. Then, I might be ready to get married.

About 30 years after the fact, I heard that Captain Steedley built a website (Swampfox.info) that included his memories of that ambush. I was surprised to find that I had been shot in the butt and shoulder during that action. I won't challenge his memories, but it didn't happen. A few years ago, I reunited with Captain Steedley and told him how unnerving it was every time we were told "five minutes" and the firepower kept getting bigger. He told me he was bluffing but was trying to hurry my ass up so we could get out of there. Believe me, I was going as fast as I could!

November 1, 1969, we (3rd Herd) got assigned to a MACV/ARVN post alongside QL19 (Tu Luong). Their assignment of keeping bridges secure along the road was failing, the bridges being rocketed every night. We were supposed to accompany them on night patrols, as an assumption was made these guys were either the VC themselves or simply going home to the local village at night. So, we did this for about four or five days. During that time, an E7 medic MACV (special forces) had unspoken, unofficial connections on post at Radcliff and in his personal brothel in An Khe (true story). Yellow bumper designations on his stolen jeep gave him unrestrained access to town and the supply depot. He "acquired" things for us that were unheard of: underwear, soft caps, M16 handgrips, beer, soda, and ice. Oh yeah, and hookers. I only know this as my duty as center for disease control for my platoon meant I had the supply of condoms. Along with my

SP-5 Ray Hubbard at LZ Hypshcol.

requested supply of condoms and med supplies, I also received 30 copies of orders unceremoniously promoting me to specialist 4th Class (I thought I had been forgotten by my HHQ guys in base camp). On one of our daily patrols, I returned to the compound to find an ARVN guy cooking some greens in a canteen cup, mixed with meat. It looked and smelled great. The meat was in chunks looking like C rat pork slices, cut into cubes. I traded him for a can of spaghetti and meatballs. When I mentioned it to one of their advisers, he told me it was probably rat meat, as earlier they were very excited about finding a rat's nest and were hunting them with slingshots.

November 5, 1969, I was sent with a squad (yeah, just a squad) of 3rd Herd guys to a secondary ARVN outpost (Dong Che) so I could perform MEDCAPs near there. While returning to that outpost after a MEDCAP, we walked through a settlement of a few shabby village huts. Pat Calhoun was there and remembers this. Damn if a guy in black pajamas took a shot at his "dinner," a freaking chicken. My "security" almost shot *him* dead. Brief apology followed as well as a peace offering of homemade rice wine, which we sipped from the dirtiest cups and saucers I've ever seen. Meanwhile, mama-san proceeded to behead, pluck, and boil the two chickens papa-san brought home. We were invited to dinner. Not for me, it was

A bell boy at Ray Hubbard's room in Sydney.

turning dark and myself and three guys returned to the compound. The other three guys came later. On another day, a girl came screaming down a small hill from her hooch saying "boxie, boxie," and pointing to her hooch. I went alone (dumb) to see if I could help. Outside the door was a small corral with a massive pig in it, covered with a blanket. She lifted up the blanket to reveal several bullet holes, dabbed with iodine. I declined treatment so she escorted me inside. The pig should have been some sort of red flag, but stupid me, I went inside. I met papa-san and through communication failures, I thought she was about to trade for pig medication when she removed her pants. It turned out to be some sort of rash, which I gave her something for, and beat it out of there, back to my squad.

November 6, 1969—this date and whereabouts I am sure of. I turned 21 that day. At someone's suggestion, I had an ARVN run to town on his motorcycle and bring me some doughnuts. Happy birthday. A few days and MEDCAPs later, the remainder of the 3rd Platoon joined us, followed by resupply helicopters. Outside the compound a mamma-san had meticulously laid out rice, shoulder to shoulder, side by side on a concrete pad about 20 by 20 feet. The labor that must have brought that about was whooshed away by a helicopter overshooting where I wanted him to land. In this approximate time frame, my medical platoon leader came to visit and count my morphine and arrange for my R&R. I had so much field seniority, I could have any location, any date. I chose Sydney, the week before Christmas.

Mid–November 1969, this incident may be incorrectly placed. We (3rd Platoon) were called to secure a Loach helicopter that had gone down. Two of them were in a hunter-killer team teasing bad guys by skimming treetops when one pilot was shot. He landed on a riverbank and was evacuated by the second pilot. We arrived and put up a perimeter around it. A Cobra gunship flew near us for support. I couldn't hear or see what they were talking about, but I heard the radio tell us, "You have little people about 100 yards in front of you, I'm going to expend a little Class 5." All of a sudden, he let go of miniguns and rockets, and I had this tremendous elation I wasn't on the business end of that. When a Huey chopper came to lift the Loach, they dropped a harness and gave us instructions to hook it up. The noise and riverbank sand blast were awful, and being as the RTO was busy, I jumped up to do the hookup. I heard the radio announce, "Don't put your foot on the windscreen," just as my leg went through it. The damn things are plastic. Who knew?

I received a box of med supplies, with an included set of orders promoting me to SP-5. No ceremony. In fact, I thought it was an error, being less than a month from the previous promotion and nobody told me squat.

Thanksgiving '69, we somehow ended up at Camp Ernari for a hot Thanksgiving meal, and for dessert, we loaded up trucks and headed up a road several miles to establish LZ Hipshoot in coordination with 1/69 armor (155s again). The armor guys supplied the mess tent for the first week, but 1/8 mess came later. During the transition, we ate C rations. However, my dad had sent me a Thanksgiving meal in the mail (I remember a canned turkey and a two-burner Sterno stove, canned cranberry sauce, and some traditional candy). C rations weren't that awful. Canned pears were a favorite, except they came in the same box with scrambled eggs and bacon. Yes, really, eggs and bacon in a can. Canned spaghetti or ham and beans weren't bad. Beans and meatballs, mixed with the cheese, was excellent. Gary Lysne used to mix the peanut butter and jelly and put it on the crackers. So innovative it was, he was going to invent it when he got home. But when he got home, Goobers had just hit store shelves. LRP rations were a freeze-dried meal to which hot water was added. They were so rare, we only got them two or three times. Four varieties, chicken with rice, chili, spaghetti, and something else. Lightweight, easy to carry, and prepare. As a morale booster, the battalion commander decided that on Wednesdays, when the clerks and jerks in base camp had chicken and mashed potatoes, he would serve them C rations, and the chicken would go to the field units. I think this happened twice, but that "meal" was packed into steel coolers or artillery canisters and dropped from a helicopter. Drinking water from an artillery canister is one thing, but mashed potatoes? It was a noble idea, however. I mentioned having beer and soda, but it wasn't always cold. Our company owned a large metal icebox that was forwarded to us anytime the company was assigned to a firebase type position for over two days. We were glad to see that, knowing it was beer and soda and knowing we were staying put for at least a while. Another twist to C rations was hoping people at home sent you condiments in the mail. My dad way oversupplied me. Also, magazines we periodically received were published specifically for the Asian theater military. There were PX ads, and you could request from Tabasco company a "C ration cookbook." Cute idea, but many ingredients other than the C rations themselves were unavailable. About this time, I was transitioned to be D Company head medic but remained with the 3rd. I inherited a .45 pistol that was handed down from the previous company medic. The serial number was scratched off (as it was stolen), and I couldn't hit anything with it.

Mid-December '69, prior to my R&R, my replacement in 3 Herd was Jay Volpe. As I moved on to become head company medic, he covered both 2nd and 3rd Platoons. I made my way to Cam Ranh Bay to go to Sydney via commercial Flying Tiger Line. The previous flight from Pleiku to there was a C-130 no-frills aircraft. I purchased my limit of two cartons of cigarettes ($2.20 each) and the preboarding limit was only two packs. I scurried around, finding nonsmokers, and dispersed two packs to each. Arrival in Melbourne, it was announced *no* cigarettes were to enter the terminal. A trash bag was passed, and the plane was sprayed, followed by a drug-sniffing dog. Between Melbourne and Sydney, I met a guy (Daniel, a supply clerk somewhere in 4th Division) who agreed to share a hotel room with me and split expenses. It turned out to be a suite at the Texas Tavern, in the Kings Cross area. My room overlooked Sydney Harbor. We rented civilian clothes for the week and stocked the room's refrigerator with adult beverages. Plans for the evening were to dine in the hotel restaurant (a gorgeous steak dinner cost about $3) followed by a nightclub in the lower level of the hotel. Numerous brochures lured us to other nightlife. Every time he picked one up, he declared that should be the place to go. I refuted with, "Let's do the hotel first." He continued focusing on others being first, so I gave up and went to dinner alone. He appeared in the restaurant very

Hubbard's room overlooking Sydney Harbor while on R&R.

drunk followed by a maître d' and announced his departure to a nightclub with other guys he met. Whatever other things occurred, that maître d' told me he was about to be ejected from the hotel, for being obnoxious. I went to that nightclub in the hotel and met a gorgeous lady (Glenda Walker) who ended up being my companion for the week. In the morning, I woke up, proceeded to the bathroom through his room only to see him very asleep with a lady in bed. She told me she owned the bar he ended up at and saved his life and brought him home. Saved his life? This is gonna be good. Do tell me, lady. He had heard that in Australia, if you invert your beer glass on the bar, you are willing to fight anyone there. Turns out, that rumor was true, and he got his ass beat. She put him behind the bar until close, then drug him home. My companion and I rented a Jaguar for $15 a day, for her to go to work and us to explore Sydney, most memorably, Bondi Beach. The locals knew how to live way cheaper than tourists. Her family preceded her to a holiday retreat south of Sydney, but she had to work until the 22nd. I said farewell to her, and she went to work for a half day before going forward to meet up with her family. I got a call from her and was told to take a cab to some pub in Sydney, where I met her and her "mates" from work for a holiday drink. I went with her to meet her family. They talked funny but were very nice. We were to become pen pals. I remembered, three more months in Vietnam, 18 more in the Army someplace, and two years more of school… I cannot get involved. I failed to hear the alarm on the last morning in Sydney and got a phone call telling me I had missed the bus and I better get to the airport immediately or I was to be AWOL. Daniel was still in bed and announced he wasn't going back. I didn't argue and scrambled to gather my civvies and headed to the airport to get a refund

Hubbard rented a Jaguar for $15 a day.

and civvies deposit and convert my Aussie currency. I have no idea what happened to Daniel; however, he had encountered some hippies that were a sort of underground for guys who wanted to get "lost."

December 25, 1969, I was back in Pleiku, temporarily, promoted to battalion medic. I am not sure how that came about, but I was told to stay in the base camp aid station and not go back to D Company. In a letter home, I referred to orders assigning me to base camp sanitation—inspect latrines, showers, and mess halls, which I don't remember doing. I saw New Year there, complete with a bunk and Armed Forces Television. My New Year's date was a stray dog adopted by the med platoon named GNID (medical shorthand for gram negative intracellular diplococci, or the clap), a prevalent malady for base camp guys who got to visit town. All men in Vietnam carried a personal atropine spring-loaded shot for nerve gas prophylaxis, and at some point, the Army dictated they be destroyed. As they were turned in to the aid station, I sat at a desk and "slammed" them into the hard desktop. And then it happened… I had one upside down and upon slamming it, the needle went through my thumb. No treatment was needed. Sheesh. Another incident was in base camp Radcliff. I got a call from C Company barracks telling me to bring the strongest sedative I could find to their barracks as some guy with an M16 had gone crazy. Holy crap, I only had a month to go, and I had to deal with this? All I could find to my access was lidocaine, a very mild anesthetic. Fortunately, the MPs got there before I and my useless medicine did. During that stint in base camp, I ran into Lieutenant North, who was temporary pay officer for Delta. He asked if I had received anything for the October 30 action. The underlying attitude of everyone in combat about medals or awards was, "That and a dime will get you a cup of coffee." Such an award would have come from *my* official unit, HHQ—and they weren't there and had no idea what I had done. So, he wrote a recommendation that sounded like I was John Wayne. Very flattering, but not true. The recommendation was for a Silver Star, but when the Army put it into the proper format and considered the time delay, it was reduced to a Bronze Star. Doc Keyes got the Silver, as his recommendation was from D Company and submitted immediately. I found out later we had both been recommended for DSC (Captain Steedley was trying to overcompensate; he knew he was guilty of walking us right into that ambush), but *my* paperwork got lost completely. This was going to be hard to explain to my dad as every letter I wrote, I began with the lie, "We are in a safe area, nothing going on…" I guess I forgot he had a TV, and the war was on the 6 o'clock news every night. Soon, I was loaned back to Delta Company and sent to a Montagnard village next to an ARVN outpost, with a "Village 37" project next to it. The Army was winning the hearts and minds by training the Montagnards how to build schools, stores, and buildings. "We fight a different war" was the slogan. I was put in a building outside the perimeter of the compound and way outside my comfort zone. In the few days I was there, I only saw a few kids and an old man who had severe burns on most of his body. I don't know how he got them; I didn't want to know. The kids had fun blowing rubber gloves into balloons and eating what candy I could scavenge.

Lt. Bruce Simmons suffered from a spider bite and spent about a month recovering from a nasty streak of pus running all the way up his leg. Another incident, a man (SP-4 Robert Sprouse) came to me with a headache. Procedure called for taking his temperature, which was 108. Impossible, that's incompatible with life. I tried my backup thermometer. Still 108. I went to another platoon's medic. His thermometer also read 108. We were located where the battalion aid station was, so I took him there and they also confirmed 108. He was the sort of guy who bounced when he walked, and he bounced all the way to the helipad where he was medevaced to the rear to get diagnosed with malaria. I think he was one of two men who were returning to the field and intentionally missed helicopter lifts to our unit in the field. During that screwing-off time, the firebase they were on was overrun, and they were killed. I overheard of an incident involving Sgt. Carl Nagel, who was training new guys about claymore mines. He demonstrated removing the blasting cap, rendering it safe; however, the blast cap was still very much alive. When he demonstrated by squeezing the trigger, and holding the blasting cap in the other hand, it went off, removing his thumb and sending shrapnel into his scrotum.

February 1970: Ultimately, I ended up at my last field assignment, as a MEDCAP brigade medic. I'm not sure how that came about. I know it was near Quinhon, a large firebase occupied by South Koreans, ARVNs, and US troops. I believe it was called Hard Times but was nicknamed "The Rock." Our battalion aid

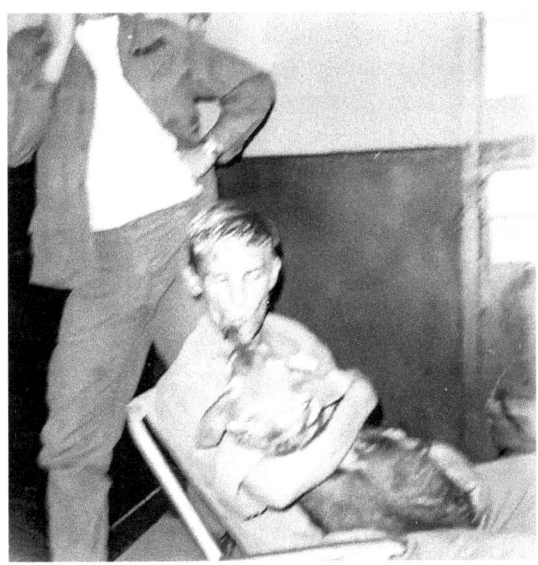

SP-5 Ray Hubbard with a stray dog adopted by Med Platoon.

doctor was there (Dr. Abijian, from Egypt) as well as battalion command. How I remember I was a brigade medic was an incident where I went to the battalion aid station to gather supplies, and Dr. Abijian told me I couldn't have them, I worked for brigade, and I had to get supply from brigade. So, I did. I made a call to brigade, and they sent a helicopter with my tiny box of Band-Aid stuff just for me. I felt like I had some real clout. I also did MED-CAPs in concert with 1/69 armor. Some days I rode to a village on an APC (armored personnel carrier), some days I walked, usually with guys not from D Company. One of the villages required a sampan float across a river. Yes, I fell into it a few times. The Koreans hated the South Vietnamese causing them to be involved in their war. For fun, I suppose, they would lob a mortar round from one side of the compound to the ARVN side. The result was a full alert the entire night, until the source was discovered. Two or three nights in a row. I was tired. On the next day's MEDCAP, we came upon a Vietnamese schmuck with a donkey by that river. Four large baskets of rice straddled that donkey, but they could conceal a mortar and rounds, so I made him dump them on the ground. I felt bad. I was wrong. On my last day in the field, I woke to gunfire sounds coming from the village I was supposed to MEDCAP that day. It wasn't appropriate to make my last day hazardous. Woo-hoo, I wasn't going to have to go ... start packing. By 10 a.m. the firefight subsided, and I was told I would go there, on foot. *Hell no.* I pulled out my brigade card and made a call to 1/69, and they sent me an APC (personnel carrier). I sat on top with all my leftover scavenged S/P junk, and we went full speed out to that village, did a 180 and full speed back. I threw out every last candy bar, shoelace, tobacco, etc., to kids standing near the road. Back on "The Rock," my next order of business was to find a way back to Pleiku. The guy on the helipad said no more birds today. Huge depression over that one. All of a sudden, a helicopter landed, with a ton of brass guys. They headed for a meeting with the battalion commander. I asked a major if I could ride back with them. It was a totally out-of-place request, but it *was* my last day. This particular helicopter had doors! And seats! I guess I begged or pleaded or maybe even cried, so he told me if I didn't mind sitting on the floor, I could go with them to An Khe. And I did. So, my next move was to figure out what to do on a helipad in Camp Radcliff. I called the 1/8 aid station, and they were going to come and get me with their jeep ambulance. At 5:00 p.m., and I was stuck halfway to my goal of Camp Ernari, Pleiku, where I could "process out." Sitting there on the edge of this "runway," in the shadow of the control tower, a three-man Loach helicopter set down and a miracle happened. The pilot walked toward me, and it turned out to be Warrant Officer Sam Gentile, a guy I was in high school with. He told me to wait five minutes for him to go to the tower and file a flight plan, and he would take me. After a bit of him "showing off" for me, I ended up in Camp Ernari, ultimately in the battalion aid station. A couple of days getting signed off on everything from the post library to the laundry and the PX, and I was on my way to Cam Ranh Bay, and home. I waited for three days for a formation to announce my name and seat assignment. Had a steak at the PX restaurant. We were on the ocean's edge. I didn't go far because they told us they never knew when extra planes/seats would become available. During a surprise formation at 10:00 p.m. on March 6, I heard my name. Pretty much it was a full night of hurry up and wait in line. We had orders, we got debriefed, we got paid, ta-da, ta-da. We were told that starlight scopes and Cobra helicopters were top secret, and we weren't to talk about them; hell, there were articles in *Time* magazine about them. I had a secret security clearance due to my access to medical records. That was another line to stand in, to be told anything I had seen in Vietnam, I was to "forget." Yeah, right.

At 6:00 a.m. we were on a bus, winding through huge walls of sandbags, and came around a corner and there it was, gloriously illuminated on a dark morning, the most beautiful glowing silver aircraft I had ever

Village 37 next to ARVN outpost used for treating Montagnards.

seen. Another Flying Tiger, complete with civilian flight attendants, 150 elated, dirty, combat-fatigued men versus five of them. When that plane lifted off Vietnamese soil, a huge gasp and roar was heard. We were on our way to Seattle via Japan and Alaska. The girls had no chance, but they had done this before and handled us very well, lots of individual talk and attention. We landed in Japan, for a routine layover, which would connect to somewhere in the Aleutians, ending in Seattle, USA. The "routine" involved some disheartening four-hour repair. To make amends, the pilot announced upon takeoff, "Sorry for the delay, guys, but as long as we were at it, we topped off the tanks and we're going straight to Seattle."

Apology accepted. We landed at approximately 6:00 a.m. in the land of the free at the same time, same day, we left a combat zone halfway

Vietnamese child Hubbard and his platoon were aiding in a village.

Sampan used to get medics to one of the villages. Soldiers unknown.

around the world (after 18 hours of flying time). Damn, if I wasn't going to be home in New York for dinner! My first flight to NYC was canceled and cost me dearly. I actually got to New York City five minutes after the last flight to Syracuse left. My duffel bag and I sat in an empty terminal (as pissed as I was the night on the mountain) watching a janitor vacuum and empty ashtrays. But, I was in the "world," and by 10:00 a.m. the next day, I was back in a snowy Syracuse (with a great tan). Upon meeting with Sharon, she told me I had changed. Yeah, I guess I did.

Looking back, I can say I did the best I could with what knowledge, skills training, and materials I had. It was true trial by fire. My assessment is that it was totally inadequate, but I did it. Thankfully, no Purple Heart, they missed me! Forty or so years later, I am amazed at the respect medics had. We were the guys that were coming to get them, no matter how, or what danger we faced. "The louder you yell, the faster we come." Every time I speak to a vet, I get a second hug, or "thank you." But those guys had the guns and kept the bad guys away so we could do our job. I know the meaning of the phrase "I got your back." Those 30 or so guys were my home for a year. They were my job. My family.

It wasn't love of country (but I do), and it wasn't to stop the spread of communism.

The following men have had reunions in the past few years in North Carolina: Capt. Ted Yamashita, Lt. Bob Ponzo, Capt. Frank Thomas, Lt. John Nolan, SSG Gary Lysne, SSG Glen Sattler, and myself. They still call me "Doc." I don't think they ever knew I had a first name.

Four

SP-4 Leo Flory, I–Corps Area North and West of Hue, 1968–69

B Company, 2nd-501, 101st Airborne Infantry

Armed Service, Vietnam Service, Good Conduct, Air Medal, Bronze Star, Combat Medical Badge, Honorary Air Assault Badge from the 101st Airborne Division Association

As I think back about it, my anxious curiosity to get over there was seriously blinded by youth. But, on August 4, I was on my way. Four days later I arrived at Cam Ranh Bay (pronounced like "Cam Ranh Bay"), in the ll Corps area of South Vietnam. The trip to Vietnam took a full 24 hours from Fort Lewis, Washington, through Anchorage, Alaska, and Yucota, Japan, and finally to Vietnam.

Cam Ranh Bay was on the coast of the South China Sea, at about the middle of the country. The landing strip at the airbase looked like it was on a long skinny sandbar that stretched out into the bay. When we landed on the PSP (preformed steel plank) runway, I could see the water almost below the wings, the bay from the left side of the plane and the ocean on the right. Landing on the corrugated steel runway caused a vibration through the entire plane until we taxied to a stop.

We were all very tired and weary from the long trip and wanted to exit the plane as soon as possible. But we were ordered to stay put until further notice. With the engines shut down, there was no air-conditioning. So, they opened two side doors to let the 100-degree humid air in. We remained baking in the hot sun for nearly two hours before two Vietnamese military men did a walk-through inspection of the fresh troops in sweat-soaked khakis and on the verge of passing out.

As soon as they finished, we were allowed to leave the plane. Some of the men were having difficulty from dehydration.

We then needed to hoof it for a mile or two to wood-framed, screened-in holding barracks that were painted white. White wooden sidewalks ran

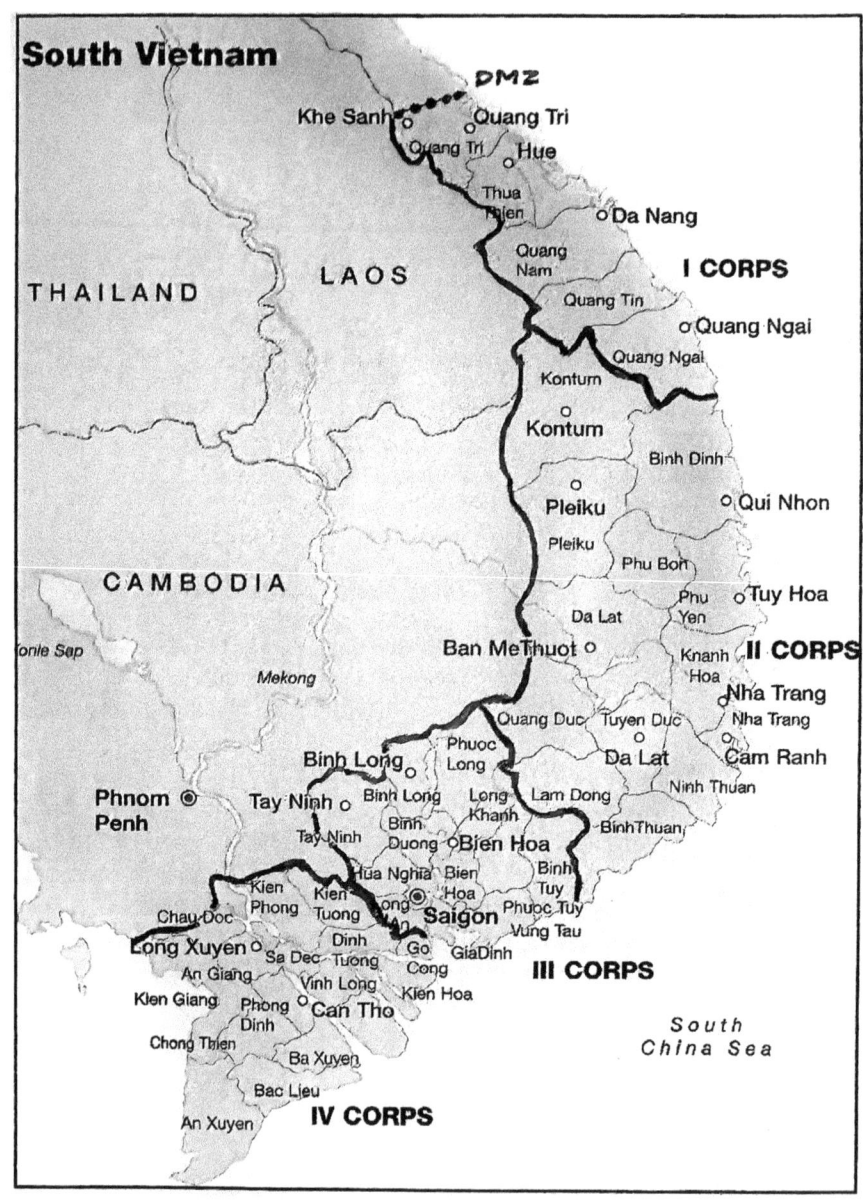

Map of Vietnam.

through the nearly white sand from building to building. That made it easy to walk, but what on earth was that weird bad smell?

Cam Ranh Bay was actually a beautiful place, tropical with palm trees and a nice breeze always coming off the ocean. If the remainder of the country was anything like this, I thought, everything should work out just fine.

Besides, my cousin Bill had already been here for six months as a helicopter mechanic, and maybe I would be stationed nearby. Within 20 hours I was in a C-130 transport plane headed for Tan Son Nhut (pronounced like "Ton Sa Nhut") Airbase, near Saigon. We boarded buses shortly after landing and caravanned through the outskirts of the city to a huge base called Bien Hoa (pronounced like "Ben Waw") in the III Corps area. We joined many other men there at the airfield, and all were ushered into a large flat-roofed open-air pavilion. There were small "hooches" (slang for house) on three sides, displaying signs with military insignias and manned by one or two men each.

Most of us were seated on plank benches, duffel bags in hand, listening to the speaker blaring out individuals' names and which unit (hooch) to report to. In due time, my name and service number were announced (along with a strange surprise), "Report to the 101st Airborne Division." "What the hell," I thought to myself, "I am not jump qualified." I had not been in the Army six months, but I already knew plenty about the airborne units, the 82nd, 173rd, and the 101st Airborne. Parachute school or jump school, as it is called, was even a prerequisite for Special Forces. "Why on earth would they be calling me to that unit? They are the most famous unit in the Army! They have made a mistake!"

I made my way over to the marquee with the large painted symbol of the 101st "Screaming Eagle Patch" and said to the attendant, "Sorry, boys, you've made a mistake, I'm not jump qualified!" "It doesn't matter," he said, "you're property of the 101st now, so just get on that truck." Next thing I know, I'm at the unit rear of the 101st Airborne Division, going through its five-day version of "Welcome to Vietnam" they called "P" training (probably because you were quite likely to pee your pants at least once before they were finished with you). It was carried out by GIs who had already done hard time with combat units, and some were still recovering from wounds.

We were immediately sent to quartermaster supply and issued new jungle fatigues, boots, baseball cap, rucksack, and most of the gear we would need for field duty. We were required to bring civilian clothing for a future R&R (rest and recuperation). That, along with our khaki uniforms and all other personal junk, was stashed in our duffel bags, tagged, recorded, and put in a warehouse. As we were in line playing follow the leader from one supply building to the next, I entered a building where M-16 rifles were being issued. It was my turn at the counter, and the attendant already had the next weapon on the counter with the barrel straight up. I quickly said that I was not qualified through the Army to carry a weapon. He shoved it out closer to me and said, "You're in Vietnam now, do you want this f—king gun or not?" I left the building with a brand-new M-16, serial number 704097X. I remember the number yet today.

By day two, the rigorous training started. All the items we were issued had to be put in the rucksack and carried nearly everywhere we went. They ran us in the morning, in midday, in the evening, and in the middle of the night, especially if it was raining. In between, we took classes on the M-16, shot up clip after clip of ammo, learned night-firing methods, and finally qualified on targets. They put us on trails, much like we might encounter in the field, and set booby traps that would explode artillery simulators if we tripped them. They had ARVN (Army of the Republic of Vietnam) troops dressed like VC (Vietcong) and ambushed us every chance they had. Everyone had to walk point (first in line) at one time or another.

Along with the tough physical training, there were classes on the culture of the country, language, civil diplomacy, and personal hygiene. Of course, we got more shots for disease prevention, and we were well warned of the dangers of venereal disease. They even had us go through a 10-minute brushing of our teeth with some new chemical that was supposed to help prevent cavities. It was called fluoride.

Let me tell you, that was the hardest, most rigorous day-and-night, intense, true-to-life, miserable training I had ever received in the military. At some point, every day, they would end up shooting very close "at us" with live ammunition in real jungle-style survival. I was enlightened before "P" training was over, and I thank the unit and the individual men that put us through that week of hell, trying to prepare us for the true hell to come.

My next set of orders was to report to LZ Sally (Landing Zone Sally), which was about 40 miles south of the DMZ (Demilitarized Zone), and the battalion rear for Second Battalion 501 Infantry Brigade, 101st Airborne Infantry Division (2/501s, 101st). Sally sounds tame enough, and it was for me, but not for the men that secured the area a few months prior to my arrival.

Traveling with the military in Vietnam turned out to be nothing less than hitchhiking. As long as you had orders, you could climb on anything with enough space going your way and ride along. I caught a C-130 to Da Nang then a deuce-and-a-half (a two-and-a-half-ton truck) headed north. It was about 15 miles of rough gravel highway into Hue City (pronounced "Way City"), which had recently been liberated and had plenty of evidence of the battles. Then came another 15 miles of what you could call "mud bogging" in a two-and-a-half-ton truck full of GIs with locked-and-loaded weapons.

Sally was a well-fortified camp with good perimeter bunkers and lots of concertina wire (huh, there is that smell again), lots of gun batteries,

105 howitzers, and even some track-mounted eight-inch guns. The housing was tents in haphazard rows with dirt or pallet floors. I felt far less safe here but was hoping this was home. That was not to be the case. I located headquarters for the 2nd Battalion and was quickly assigned to "B" Company, which was in the field doing "recon" (reconnaissance) in the vicinity. I already had a rucksack, steel pot, M-16, and other field gear. I got my field aid bag from the medical supply hooch, and a veteran medic helped me stock it quite well. I spent the evening trying to make sense of all the gear, got it packed and tied down as best I could, then slept on a wooden pallet that night.

Next morning, I had my first breakfast of C rats (C rations) and got promptly put on "Shit Detail." "What's 'Shit Detail'?" I asked. "Why, all newbies get to do it," he said, and he had me carry two five-gallon cans of diesel fuel to the back of the outhouse area. I was instructed to prop open the back door, use a rebar hook to drag out the sawed-off 50-gallon drums full of shit and urine, pour in some diesel fuel, light it on fire, and stir it occasionally with a fence stake until the contents were gone. I soon found out where that weird smell came from!

Another interesting thing about sanitary control on almost every base is that in almost every conceivable place, you could find a "piss tube." They were made from aluminum canisters that held howitzer rounds. They had a rim at the opening that worked well at holding a piece of bug screen. Just knock a hole in the other end and bury it at a slight angle, about a foot into the ground. If you were on a base, you never had to walk very far to take a leak. By noon that day, I was getting my first UH-I helicopter ride out to B Company along with a load of C rations, water, assorted ammunition, and a bag of mail.

B Company was in a defensive position about three or four miles out from Sally and was taking on supplies for a five-day hike. I was assigned to 3rd Platoon and introduced to some of the guys. Shortly thereafter we were on foot and looking for Charlie (slang for "enemy"). Now, things were starting to get a little scary, and a taste of reality was stinging my palate.

Infantry (all divisions) has one basic job, and that is to "seek out the enemy, make contact with him, kill or capture him, and take his stuff." It seemed, however, that the 101st had a reputation to uphold in this regard: the more ground you can cover, the more likely you are to make contact.

Now, I was in extremely good condition. But after humping close to a hundred pounds of gear a good six klicks (slang for kilometers) through the rice paddies, thickets, and bamboo, my butt was kicked at the end of the day. We dug in, had a hasty meal of C rats, and prepared for dark, always a "scary time." I talked to a guy that night about our hike and asked if they did that very often. He said that today had been a short day because of receiving supplies and that tomorrow would be longer. "Ten klicks a day, it's the airborne way, hurrah."

The next day he got to me quickly, went through my pack, and tossed out everything that I did not need. We gave the stuff a shallow grave, and my equipment was about 15 pounds lighter. The "grunt" who helped me was Danny (Snake) Wakefield, from Minnesota. He had joined the unit about 30 days before. He kept me under his wing for some time, and we have remained good friends to this day. As the days wore on, I met many other good and brave men, like Garry Welch of Iowa, Jimmy Green of Texas, Mel Waite, Bob Baldwin, Larry Trask, and Joe Hudson of Michigan, "Gap" (Dale Fisher, from Pleasant Gap, Pennsylvania), Pat O'Leary from Manhattan, Robert Butts from Detroit, David Krautscheid from Oregon, David Reinheimer of St. Louis, Missouri, Al Kontrabecki from Niagara Falls, Irvin (Moose) McCouan from Montana, Frank Hilly and Patrick Armendariz from California, Jackie Johns from Iowa, and many, many others. All these men took their turns walking on point or humping the "60" (slang for M-60, the .30-caliber machine gun), also known as "The Pig."

We worked the lowland rice paddies, small hamlets, and farms, farther and farther away from Sally, from September to December, without making contact with the enemy. There was one exception to that. A Vietcong soldier became a "chiew-hui" (defector, pronounced "chu hoy") and walked toward our NDP (night defensive position) one morning with a white rag tied to a stick and gave himself up. We treated him well, humped him out to the nearest road, where we were met by an MP (military police) truck that took him to who knows where. At that point in time, the area from Da Nang through Hue to Quang Tri was basically cleared of enemies, all the way west beyond the rice paddies to the foothills. We humped our 10K per day, rooting through everything that showed promise, but found no Charlie. Of course, no one had a problem with that. We did, however, find several large caches of weapons, which gave us some notoriety.

I became accustomed to my job of "making the rounds" and did what I could for the guys with cuts, boils, jungle rot, foot problems, and bug and leech bites. Sometimes immediate action was required; otherwise just the normal evening ritual. Once a week, after LOG (short for logistics supply) day, I passed out enough anti-malaria pills to each platoon sergeant for all his men at one per day. They were in tiny foil packets on a roll like raffle tickets, and I gave them out in groups of six for each guy. Also included in this was a large orange pill, as part of the regimen that I gave out personally every Monday. The guys would not take them otherwise because it meant it was loose bowel Tuesday. These rituals never stopped during the length of my full field duty.

By now, my curiosity about Vietnam had waned a bit, and a little bit of a chip began to grow on my shoulder. I was drafted, I could be home making some good money and chasing the babes around town. There was some evidence of the hippie movement and anti–American tactics of academia in regard to the war, but we were isolated from most of it. The magic '60s were a spectacular time to be a teenager in America and, well, what were we doing here? I could have been a better soldier at that time. We "humped" (walking with full field gear) from early morning to evening every day, allowing just enough time to dig in, string up a quick hooch, and eat a few C rats. During these long reconnaissance missions, we were in and around many rice paddies, fording rivers, and streams almost daily. The waters in these paddies and lowland areas were full of leeches, big ones. You could see them swimming like snakes toward you. Hunting for Charlie, humping heavy packs, and fighting the heat, leeches, mosquitoes, flies, and muddy wet feet and clothes was our daily grind. The water was bad, too. Every canteen needed pellets of halazone added to decontaminate it. It was also my job to make sure the men had plenty of it and that they used it in their water. It tasted like shit, but it would keep you from getting sick.

We were in the field almost continuously, but occasionally we pulled perimeter guard duty on a firebase. For us that was a good feeling of safety. We could sleep in preconstructed sandbag and PSP bunkers, and sometimes they didn't leak much when it rained. During one of these extended field tours, we met up with several of our sister companies along a canal that led into Hue. We set up a cordon line that stretched out, possibly a klick, down to the water's edge. It was like driving deer at the end of the hunting season. We held a line while a sister company attempted to flush out any enemy in the dense vegetation on the opposite side of the river.

The canal was 50–80 feet across and fairly deep. We were on an ancient dredging along the bank, covered with short grass that looked like a pasturing area for water buffalo. The dredging sloped off away from the canal and into the rice paddies that were almost endless. It was easy duty for a couple of days, almost like being on a picnic. It didn't matter if we made noise during the day. I was introduced to a model 1911, .45-caliber automatic pistol, and several of us wasted some ammunition plunking anything we could see across the river.

Farther downstream, either at the end of our company or the beginning of the next, the guys pulled concertina wire across the river to stop any sampans (boats) and search them. The 3rd Platoon was at the far upstream end of the line, and we were not aware of what was happening at the barricade until we saw a medevac helicopter fly in, set down for a moment, then leave again. The word filtered down to us eventually that one of the GIs stringing the wire had decided to cool off when the work was done. He dove off the borrowed sampan into the canal but did not return to the surface. He became tangled in wire that had sunk to the bottom at some previous cordon. The four-minute grace period had long passed before his comrades could pull him free and get him back on land.

After three months of hard pounding without one man lost to enemy fire, some unwitting grunt tries to escape the heat, drowns, and becomes our first casualty. We were all sick in the gut for some time after that. The second day a sampan was spotted navigating down the river toward Hue with a very old man and woman on board. A four-striper (staff sergeant) I'll call Sgt. D.A. flagged the old handmade craft to shore. They had one large sack of rice with them. Sgt. D.A. started yelling at them, interrogating them in English and pointing at the bag of rice. He directed them off the boat by waving his .45 pistols toward shore, climbed in, slit the bag of rice, and dumped it in the water. It was easy to see the complete and utter fear and disbelief in their eyes as they climbed back in the sampan and retreated slowly back the way they came, having never uttered a sound the entire time. I asked Sgt. D.A. why he did that. He explained that they were most likely trying to get the rice to the VC. I replied that they were headed into Hue, where any VC could get all the rice he wanted. I wasn't a military strategist, but I would have been more skeptical if a sampan were headed upstream deep into the bush. What I think we did was dump out their means of subsistence for the next six months. You are free to decode the meaning of D.A. Another time we NDP'd (night defensive positioned) around a small, very old, and decayed pagoda. It had enough space inside to hold the CP (command post), and we slept on the smooth stone floor. My guard duty came in the middle of the night. It was quite moonlit, and I sat on the edge of the open-air pagoda because the raised floor made a good place to sit. It was everyone's job to pull night watch for one to two hours, with the "Pric 25" (radio) mic in hand. Every 15 minutes or so you would quietly say, "1st squad, sit rep negative, break squelch twice," and so on for 2nd and 3rd platoons.

As long as the platoon guard depressed the mic key twice, causing a small audible sound, all was well. Mosquitoes ruled the night, and flies took over for the day shift. As I sat in the quiet moonlight, I could hear mosquitoes buzzing ever more intently, but I couldn't see them. This went on for a while, becoming more and more noisy! I had my legs held close together, supporting the radio mic, and at some point, I grabbed the mic to make a "strep request." I spread my legs and a cloud of mosquitoes poured upward into the moonlight that they must have been trying to avoid, or it was warm under my legs. The tiny mystery was solved, and I kept my legs spread wide. I continued to sit quietly on guard, almost enjoying the peaceful night and the strange old religious icon we were in. Then from the corner of my eye, I saw movement, not in the perimeter but just at the edge of the cut-stone slab I was sitting on. Rolling my eyes down slowly, I spied a giant snail that was at least 4" across the shell and 6 or 7" long slowly moving toward me. He was a great distraction for my last hour on guard. Now I understood why the French eat escargot because this sucker would have fed four people. My guard duty over, I slept well the remainder of the night.

By November we had worked into the foothills and made our first company helicopter lift into the edge of the northern highland, to a firebase called T-Bone. We had a great east visual to Sally from the FB (firebase). We spent about a week pulling perimeter guard at night and made sweeps farther and farther out from the base during the day. The terrain was quite hilly with occasional trees, but mostly low underbrush.

One morning, movement was spotted about two klicks down the hill; five or six people were moving around down below. The artillery guys had binoculars, and we glassed them for a while. A squad (me included) led by Sgt. D.A. was dispatched down the hill to see what they were doing. The squad traveled very light, but I always needed to carry a full pack because the aid bag was heavy and secured well to my backpack frame. As we approached, it became evident that they were old women with small chopping knives working their way across the hill and gathering a local weed-like willow tree that would grow four- or five-foot stalks slightly larger than a pencil in diameter. I had been in a few small villages by then and recognized that it was the fuel that all the rural people used for cooking. They dried out bundles of the stuff, hung on or inside the homes. When broken up by hand into pieces six to 10 inches long, it made a nice hot fire they controlled by adding sticks as needed. It also had a very nice aroma when burned.

It was also easy to tell that the area had been "farmed" for this resource for many years. Nonetheless, out comes sergeant D.A.'s .45. He waved it at the women's heads, screaming "Dedie-mow, dedie-mow" ("Go away"). These women actually looked pissed off, but again, not saying a word, they picked up their meager collection and headed home. God only knows how far away that was. We were at a great visual advantage point from T-Bone, and I couldn't see any villages from there. Sgt. D.A. happened to be a Black man, which had no bearing on what he was doing. It was just the way he was, "Old Army."

I learned to dislike the guy. The issue was not prejudicial, but I will touch on that matter later. While on FB T-Bone, I was chewing gum one day and managed to pull out an old filling from a tooth. There were regular flights back and forth to Sally, and the platoon leader was sitting on the empty floor. We leaned against the back wall of the ship that divided the cargo area from the door gunners and relaxed for the ride. Most Hueys had the doors removed, and there was not much to hang on to inside. You just relied on gravity and a little "stick shin" to stay in the craft. The pilot cranked her up, lifted off as normal, flew off the base a short distance, and put the bird in a steep dive down the side of the hill. Ooowwweee, that bird gained speed fast. Down the big hill, over several foothills, flying too close to the ground for my comfort, the pilot, laughing his butt off, held the bird at full throttle across four miles of rice paddies, straight to Sally. We were actually leaving wake in the water as he cranked that bird all the way to the perimeter, then jerked the collective back as hard as he could, making a near straight-up climb until the bird nearly stalled. The pilot then made a couple of nice easy circles down to the PSP landing zone and softly touched down. As the pilot and crew continued laughing, I am saying "Holy bat shit" (famous Danny "Snake" Wakefield quote). What a ride! I found the dentist's hooch along with his hydraulic chair and foot-pedal-operated drill, but no dentist. I caught a nice uneventful ride back to T-Bone that evening and never got that tooth fixed until I was back in the States.

Bob Baldwin had a camera while on T-Bone and took lots of pictures. He took one of me and Jimmy Green standing near the perimeter. Jimmy was a year or so older than the rest of us and must have had a dozen girlfriends. He always received more perfume-soaked letters than anyone, good care packages too. At our 2009 reunion, Bob presented me with a framed copy of that photo, which I had long forgotten about, and I am so happy to have it now. We were sent to guard FB Birmingham for the first time. It was about 14 miles southwest of Hue and had road access from route #547, which eventually led through the Ashau Valley and into Laos.

Birmingham was in a fairly secure area with very nice bunkers and a few wood-frame barracks that the arty (artillery) and engineer guys stayed in. Some weeks earlier, while out on mission, A Company came across a 16-foot python. They caught it, put it in a mail sack, and humped that thing on a pole until they had perimeter duty on Birmingham.

The engineers built a very nice chicken wire cage for that serpent and supplied it with ducklings (big as small chickens) to snack on. Well, me and old Danny (Snake) Wakefield had a few extra beers one day and decided that the python needed to eat one of the ducks. Dan got the python's head while I caught a duckling. Dan found that if he squeezed the snake's neck hard enough, it would open its mouth. "Holy bats, what a mouth." I made several attempts at trying to stuff the frantic bird into the python's mouth when I noticed (wits dimmed by the beer) that the majority of the snake's body was sneaking out of the cage and gently beginning to hug old Dan. Dan's eyes got pretty big when he realized what was happening. I quickly returned the duck to the cage and began the fight with Mr. Wiggly. Those suckers are far stronger than you'd think. We had a heck of a time getting him back in the cage. As we were guarding another FB called Boyd, A, C, and D Companies managed to score the first contact with the enemy since late summer. They were on top of a high jungle ridge farther south and west from FB Boyd, and they didn't just make contact, they stirred up a first-class hornets' nest. The radio traffic was heavy for several days. They were taking casualties, a lot of them.

It was late November or early December when orders came from the commander, Captain Hallums. I do not remember him, as I did not have many opportunities to travel with the company command post in those early months. And that also was about the time that the command was taken over by Captain Graney, whom I grew to know fairly well as time passed. "Saddle up, B Company, we're going to help our sister companies." Our cream puff times in the field were coming to an end.

On day one of this mission, we all knew it was likely to get more serious as we headed out in six-bird sorties, taking one platoon at a time out to their hand-chopped LZ, which was on a very high and continuous ridge that divided the highlands from the lowlands. I don't remember which lift I was on. There were a lot of guys in the woods all around the LZ when I arrived. With a new and unfamiliar look on their faces, they were slump-shouldered and hollow-eyed. Men from these units were boarding the birds as we were getting off. We were quickly mustered up and headed south, along the ridgeline where much of the action had taken place. We learned that a Huey had been hit the day before, crashed through the canopy and caught fire. We came across two pairs of grunts with poles over their shoulders, ponchos tied to the poles, and the charred remains of two crew members in each one. There were morbid looks on the men whose duty it was to dig out the overcooked remains of their bodies from the burnt-out fuselage, after it cooled down through the night (I think my gray matter has blocked out any memory of the smell that permeated the area that day). Two of the bodies were fused together. It appeared that a door gunner made a heroic effort to free one of the pilots. He made it to the door, opened it, and tried to free him, but they burned to death together. B Company made its way far beyond the other units, using a newfound form of stealth. The afternoon was uneventful, and we dug in for the night on that razorback ridge. We were headed out of the NDP early the next morning, reconnoitering the ridge, slowly moving forward. The guys were on their toes and spotted movement ahead. They brought a M-60 gunner to the point position. Sure enough, it was a "gook" sneaking along the trail toward our position, and the machine gunner took him down. The remainder of the day was uneventful, but B Company had a body count for the first time in five months.

Day two of that mission took us down a steep crevasse, deep into the jungle. With extreme stealth and cautious "point recons," we moved down into valley. We were into triple-canopy jungle for the first time now. Midafternoon, the company came to a halt. The point men had discovered an area full of thatched huts. We cased the area carefully, then moved in to scout each hooch, 10 to 12 in all. About 30 minutes passed, when someone shouted out, "Booby traps in the doorways!" Everyone came to a paralyzing halt, then pulled bayonets, prodded the ground at the entrances, and, sure enough, there were 60 mm mortar rounds buried at the center of each opening. Fortunately for us, the enemy had neglected to remove the safety caps from the explosive devices.

We spent the remainder of that day and all of the next day sweeping the area around the enemy camp. We found that the hooch farthest down the hill was a cook shack. It had a rather elaborate dirt hearth with a large aluminum bowl of rice still on it and still warm. The rice, mixed with some sort of starchy tuber, was quite good, by the way. We discovered that they dug a trench from the hearth up the hill and under the floor of most of the hooches. They covered the entire length of it with thatch and dirt to prevent smoke from rising up and marking their location. They had a small hatch door in each hut that allowed a little smoke to filter through the thatch roofs. All of this was made from jungle materials. One hooch was, no doubt, a briefing pavilion, with a place to hang maps or whatever on the wall and even a piece of visqueen fixed into the roof as a skylight.

There was a small tumbling stream working its way down through the camp, and the guys eventually found the entrance to a cave dug 40–50 yards back into the hillside. The NVA (North Vietnamese Army) piled the dirt into the stream, which washed it far downstream so there was no mining slag left to be seen by the allied forces flying over. There was a small but significant cache of weapons, mortar rounds, and ammunition in the cave, which we hauled out and packed along with us. It was raining when we left the camp on day four, and I was given a 20-pound sack of 7.62 rounds (standard bullet for the Russian-built AK-47) and told to scatter them as we made our way slowly up the hill via a different route. Like Johnny Appleseed, I scattered the rounds through the jungle until the sack was empty.

The drizzle continued, and about midday the column came to a halt with the hand signal given to be very quiet. Movement was spotted on top of a knoll, and the .60 gunner was once again deployed to point. He maneuvered to a vantage point and killed two more NVA. The dead NVA were dressed in khaki uniforms and had fresh haircuts and crude rucksacks with about six 60 mm mortars rounds in each and one AK-47 rifle. We formed a perimeter around the dead men, searched them, divided up their weapons, and ate some C rats before moving on. We worked toward the ridge we had originally come down four days earlier but did not make it to the top that day. On day five, we reached the top, but in that area, it was nearly sheer cliffs. Recon teams searched in both directions until we found a reasonable place to climb down with the assistance of rappelling rope. It took some time for every man in the company to "half-ass" rappel down the first 100 feet of that hill. How the last man untied the rope, I don't know. For the rest of that day, we slowly made our way down an extremely steep wooded area, hanging on to anything we could to keep from falling. We stopped at a point where a huge rock projected out from the face of the slope, big enough for the entire company command post, led by Capt. James Hallums, to form a night defensive position on the top. When the downward movement stopped, each man had to try his best to find a place to hang on and sleep for the night. We felt fairly safe because there was no logical reason for any enemy to be there. It was getting dark fast, and I found a nice cradle-shaped place on a projected tree root and called it good. There were 30 or 40 men above my location at the bottom of the big rock, and debris was occasionally tumbling down the slope and flying over my nest and on down the hill. All was well until I heard a large rock coming down, bounding off anything in its path, and men hollering, "Heads up, heads up." It was pitch-dark, couldn't see shit, as that rock slammed into something directly above me. All was silent for a second and, wham, that frickin' rock landed square on my gut and drove all the air from my lungs. I went brain dead for a second and pushed the rock off me, only to send it tumbling down past the rest of the company farther down from me. It didn't hit anyone else and is probably still going down that hill. I foraged around in the dark until I found a small tree jutting out well under the big rock but out of the line of falling stones. I hung my sore gut over the tree and dangled there. When you're tired enough, you can sleep even like that.

On day five, there was no way to fix a meal, so we continued to head downhill for several more hours. We abruptly reached the bottom and in short order found a very nice 30-foot-wide stream. The company commander had us form a perimeter on each side, and everyone got a chance to lie in the stream and clean up a bit. After about an hour, we "rucked up" and started a force march across the rice paddies that lasted about six or seven hours. We arrived at FB Boyd (some referred to it as Panther II) before dark. You could probably call this luck, but when we came through the perimeter of the FB a small USO (United Service Organizations) show was about to start. It was a five-piece Korean rock band doing American '60s music. We were an unshaved, raggedy, mean-looking rabble of infantry dudes who had just come from a tough and fully successful mission, as we somewhat impolitely took over all the good seating positions and enjoyed the heck out of that third-rate show. The perimeter bunkers were already under guard, so after the show we had a little free time. Several of the guys sneaked into the back of the supply tent and made off with several cases of C rats. We stripped them of the good stuff, like peaches and pound cake, then just sacked out where it looked comfortable and slept well.

The entire battalion was deployed in an area around the south end of the Ashau Valley. The valley was well known to us in the I Corps area as probably the worst possible death trap a GI would ever want to enter. We knew we were close to it but thank God we weren't in it.

When leaving Sally, we assaulted into an area of very big hills and began hunting for the enemy. On January 20 we were working our way down a hill, stopping to recon every 10–15 minutes. Going was tough, as it was an extraordinarily steep hill and under triple canopy. I remember coming to a place where the trail turned a hard left, followed the slope horizontally, and made a nice flat place to walk for about 50–60 feet. The sun came through a large opening in the canopy above the flat area, then the trail turned right again and dropped at nearly 70 degrees downhill. I worked my way down another 100–200 feet, when the line stopped again for recon, and I pushed off to the right 20 feet or so to guard our flank. Ten minutes passed, with little or no noise other than that of nature. "Bang!" The rifle report that rang out back up the hill drilled all of us in position. Muffled voices came from above, then a message whispered from man to man came to me as "Medic needed." Nothing like this had happened before. The look of raw question appeared on the faces of the men as I passed them one by one, their safeties off, fingers on triggers, wishing they had x-ray vision. I began moving back up the trail, trying to be quiet but as quick as I could. As I reached the horizontal section of the trail, it was almost like climbing a wall, and as I peered over the edge, I could see GIs with their weapons trained toward the opening in the jungle. A GI lay on his back, only three feet away, when I climbed onto the ledge. My heart was already working hard from the climb but went into high gear when the reality sank in of seeing my good friend Jimmy Green with a large amount of blood oozing from his head and onto the ground. "Sniper," I thought, and now I am vulnerable! "God damn it, boys, keep your eyes open," I said, as I jerked off my pack and simultaneously tried to figure out what to do first. Our training at Fort Sam was designed around three basic principles: stop the bleeding—clear the airway—prevent shock. Jim was taking raggedy breaths with long pauses in between. Still on my knees, I maneuvered to his side, got hold of his shoulder, slid my left hand into the blood under his head to roll him over far enough to see the wound. As I did, my fingers sank deep into the back of Jimmy's skull, and I knew that Jimmy's condition was fatal. I grunted out, "He's gone," and laid his head back down. Having come from a rural farming and livestock area, where the slaughter of animals was commonplace, and loving the sport of hunting, on those terms I knew death. I knew I was right about Jimmy's condition. A flow of tears came, and I went into some kind of chant, like a broken record—he's gone—he's gone—he's gone. It stopped when Lieutenant Pue said sharply, "Stop it, Flory. Do whatever you can for him. The medevac is on the way." I had forgotten about the sniper who had done his work for the day and apparently left. I pulled a few appropriate bandages around his head as Jimmy's body continued to do what the involuntary muscles and nerves are supposed to do. He breathed with very long breaths even though I couldn't find a pulse. Meanwhile the guys were trying to mark our spot by popping smoke, all of which just drifted down through the forest. They finally bent down a small tree, tied a smoke grenade to it, pulled the pin, and let it spring back up into the opening. In minutes, the medevac was there, deploying a jungle penetrator (a cylindrical device with a folding seat and harness that fastens to a cable, and is lowered from a helicopter through the opening in the trees). Jim's involuntary breathing had stopped, and I was on my own to move him 25 feet or so to align with the penetrator. I needed to figure out the mechanics of the device, then fold down parts that created the seat that a rider could straddle. I had one hell of a time getting Jimmy's limp body on that thing and strapped in. But extraction began with Jim's arms hanging down and his head hung back as we began to see the shadowed side of him heading toward the opening above. When a vine found its way across his neck halfway out of the canopy, the pilot and crew (God bless those guys) lowered the cable again, maneuvered, and freed him from yet another insult before clearing the top of the jungle and pulling him on board.

The chopper left, but the radio began barking at the brass, as these medevac missions are extremely dangerous for the crew when penetrators are used. We were not supposed to use them for KIAs (killed in action), but at the same time, it would have been extremely difficult and dangerous to sling a body in a poncho strung up on a pole between two guys, navigate the mountainous country, and hunt for Charlie until the next LOG day.

Medical training at Fort Sam was very good but sorely lacking in preparing us for the rigors of combat. We had never seen a backpack aid bag, nor had been shown how to stock one. Knowing how to operate a jungle penetrator would have been handy about then. We were also taught nothing of the psychological effects of dealing with traumatically injured and dying men. Things changed for all of us that day, I think especially for me, when our first WIA (wounded in action) became KIA by the time he hit the ground. I was still a shithead kid with an attitude about being there, but Jimmy taught me what my job really was, and I resolved to do it better from that day forth and to be a better soldier. Jimmy Green from Dumas, Texas, was the icebreaker for B Company. The mission continued.

For the most part, us line doggies had no clue where we were at any given time while in the jungle, but when air assault missions took us from the places we normally frequented to fire support bases like FB Boyd, Birmingham, Bastogne, or Vehgil, we could see they all lay in a westerly direction from Hue, with the Ashau Valley beyond them. FB Boyd was a big round knob of a hill maybe 1,500 feet high. A single company could guard the perimeter. It and the others were all accessible by road. At the base were the remains of an old airstrip that was almost part of the road, but no buildings or tarmac. There had been little or no enemy activity in the area for some time, and we could relax a little while we were there. A USO show came to Boyd one time, a small Korean rock and roll band with some female singers. They were quite good, and we enjoyed the heck out of it. Another time at Christmas, most of us received care packages from home. Pat O'Leary received a small plastic Christmas tree, complete with decorations. He assembled it all beside his bunker, an area we all gathered in to eat and shoot the bull, and the little tree from home was enjoyed by all. Firebases were good places to receive LOG and good places to add on new recruits.

By now, many men of the original unit were finishing their year and heading home. We picked up a new recruit on Boyd one time, a tall, slender Native American named Clyde Cross Guns. He was shortly thereafter observed slithering around and through the rocky perimeter, peeking out here and there. We said, "Clyde, what are you doing?" He replied, "Looking for snipers!" We said, "Good idea" and let him go about his business. Later, Clyde earned our respect when he became one of the many good point men, and we all relied on him.

Vehgil had what looked like a man-made ridge through part of the camp, with bunkers built 30 feet or so down below the narrow, flat-topped ridge. Helicopters used it as an LZ and could land anywhere on the length of it. On a clear day, a Loach (small pumpkin-seed-shaped helicopter that seated two crew and two passengers) carrying two high brass landed on it and stayed for an hour or two. Later, the original occupants climbed back on board, the little chopper fired up and prepared to take off.

When the bird was warmed up, it lifted up as normal, transitioned sideways to begin flight, but apparently lost lift as it moved away from the ridge. I and others were on top of a bunker down below and in line with the craft as it lifted off. We were watching it when it disappeared over the opposite side. *"Crash"* echoed back over the ridge! At about the same time a steel pot (helmet) flew over the ridge and rolled down the slope to our bunker. It was totally smashed! My aid bag was in the CP hooch, but we all scrambled to the crash site as fast as we could go. The Loach was lying on its side atop a bunker, rotors twisted and bent, a little smoke drifting up, and it was already covered with GIs pulling the occupants free. Amazingly enough, no one was seriously hurt on the ground or in the chopper, only cuts and bruises. I had always wanted to ride on a Loach in the worst way but never got the chance.

Part of our platoon CP was put into a rather nice, almost totally buried wood-framed bunker with a wooden floor. I had an idea of constructing a raised bunk and scrounged the base for enough lumber scraps to build the bed off the floor. I laid out my poncho and poncho liner neatly on it and headed out to see if the guys needed anything.

On my return I found that a Black guy named Wooten, who was an RTO (radio transmission operator) at the time, had decided for some reason that I was below his pecking order. He had given me a great deal of shit over the last several months, and now he had thrown all my gear into the corners and was lying out on my freshly built bunk, his hands behind his head. As a big grin came up on his face when I stepped in, I looked at what he had done for a second, and all the crap he had given me over several months came out all at once. Before he could blink, I spanned the 10 feet between us. I crossed my arms into the position for mounting a rucksack, grabbed his fatigue jacket just below his collar, then jerked him off the cot in a choreographed spin, ending with him over my back in rucksack position. With everything a 145-pound Michigan farm boy could put forth, I lunged forward, bending over at the same time and throwing him against the wall some five feet away. For a split second he looked like he was standing on his head, his eyes big as barrels. He then slid on his back out onto the floor.

Wooten got up, grabbed his things, and looked at me, sputtering and stuttering. Finally, he said, "You in trouble, you in trouble, white boy!" and headed off to another bunker. I worried about it for a while. But that stopped his harassment. I think he decided not to "mess with the medic" anymore. Aside from constantly harassing me and trying to make life more miserable than it already was, Wooten was a whiner. He probably whined to another Black guy named Sergeant Battle about what the mean old medic did to him, and after that Sergeant Battle began giving me constant problems.

Battle was different, more of a tough guy who had been in the Army for a while. He was the artillery forward observer for our platoon, therefore always with the platoon CP. He never missed an opportunity to try to make my life harder. It would not have been wise to go after him physically, so I just endured, hoping he would leave the unit soon. But it's also my nature to look for another way to return a favor. Vehgil was a rough, muddy knob with one or two batteries of artillery and some sort of communication unit. Someone on that base had the clout to have a refrigerated trailer, stocked with meat and frozen vegetables, and a makeshift cook shack provided the base inhabitants one meal a day, and it beat C rats big-time. The trailer had a gas-powered refrigeration unit that ran automatically to control the temperature. On the second day I had a great idea and crawled under the trailer and hooked one end of a claymore wire to the battery, then buried the wire slightly as it ran into our bunker. After removing a taillight from the trailer, and a little handiwork with medical tape, we had an electric light in the bunker. It made a great place to write letters home.

Most of our missions would last from one to six weeks. Some lasted two to three weeks.

Before returning to a FB for "line doggies," time passes in a strange way. There are no Sundays or Tuesdays, no TGIFs, no holidays except Christmas and the Fourth of July, and for some guys, not even that. Months blended together and trouble me now as I write these lines, trying to put things in chronological order. I can remember the events, but when? The only thing a pocket calendar was good for was to cross off one more day closer to going home and, of course, for marking the seven-day intervals between handing out the big, orange malaria pills.

Most missions would begin with a full-company assault, which then split into three platoons of about 30 men each. Sometimes we would meet for an NDP, then head out in separate directions again.

On occasion the 3rd Platoon was given a dog handler with a German shepherd. These guys were always more than willing to walk point. We were encroaching closer and closer into Charlie's supply routes. We saw paths being obviously used along with other clues of human activity. We broke camp early as usual one morning, and, for whatever reason, we headed back out in the same direction we had come into the NDP site the night before. The dog handler moved out about 200 feet, while the rest of us were rucking up and slowly moving into the line.

As he told the story later, a gook literally jumped out of a thicket, took a quick bead, and shot an RPG (rocket-propelled grenade) directly at him. He had one split second to dodge the rocket, but in the process his right forearm, cradling his M-16, caught the rear fin of the rocket, cutting a deep gash from his wrist to his elbow. The RPG deflected into a bush and exploded. The sound of the detonation marked the start of the ambush, as one or two AK-47s cut loose in our direction.

Almost instantly, the men in the point line returned fire, and in a few seconds those that were remaining in the NDP had jumped to the perimeter and opened fire to protect the flanks. Seconds after that, an M-60 was pounding the area the ambush came from. They "lit up" the area fairly well, then several men charged the spot. But the gooks must have immediately turned and run behind a berm and down a gulch that protected them from the onslaught.

When I got to the dog handler, he was shaken up but laughing at how close he had come to his end. We didn't carry sutures in the bush, and he needed stitches bad, but we were not going to head for an LZ for three more days. I used about 20 butterfly bandages to close the wound, a few good compresses, and a roll of Ace wrap, and he was back on point. There was no body count on either side, but it may have been on this same mission that the dog sniffed out and discovered one hell of a cache of weapons. Just covered up with thatch were 100 or more long guns, AK-47s, old bolt-action rifles, as well as 60 mm mortar tubes, a couple of old light machine guns, and a small amount of ammunition. The entire cache was divided up between all of us and carried some distance to a location where we chopped out an LZ, and the weapons were flown back to Sally.

Days turned into weeks, and big hills turned into mountains as the jungle canopy grew thicker and thicker. I knew we were somewhere west of Hue, in the Thou Thin Province, but that was about it. It would happen from time to time that conditions would prevent us from finding a good NDP. The recons would continue until the point of darkness before we would stop, form the rough semblance of an NDP, crawl off the trail a short distance with a buddy or two, and try to catch a few winks during the long night. Any condition outside the confines of an established fortified base called for as much silence as possible, especially at night. But on one of these more desperate NDP nights, one of the men let out a muffled screech and cursing ensued along with thrashing in the bushes. The man was only about 20 feet from me, and I could hear him crawling in my direction, whispering to anyone in earshot as to my location. I was up on my knees by then, couldn't see my hand in front of my face, and guided the man with low tones to my spot. I recognized the man's voice as Sgt. D.A., mumbling curse words and something about, "A freaking rat bit me." What the hell, I thought, first time for everything. Finding my flashlight, I held it under my helmet to shade the light as he explained that it bit him on the forehead. I had him lay on his back and took a look. Blood was coming from two small gashes. As I cleaned them up, I asked him how he knew it was a rat. He said he grabbed the son of a bitch with both hands and tried to crush it before flinging it into the jungle. I dressed the wound as he repeatedly asked if he would get rabies. I assured him he would not, and that I would change the dressing in the daylight. I chuckled to myself as I turned to get comfortable on the foliage of the jungle floor, wondering why that rat chose ol' Sgt. D.A.

On extra-dark nights like these, I noticed tiny bits of something making a phosphorescent glow on the forest floor. I saved small sticks and leaves that I found, some brighter than others. Retrieving them the next day, I looked for the source of the light, but there was never anything to be seen. The only common clue was that the foliage was always dead and decaying. I learned over time to use the phenomenon to move around at night if I needed to get to the radio for night watch or whatever. I found that I could distinguish objects 25 to 30 feet away.

If my memory serves me correctly, Wooten was still with the platoon. He hated the ground I walked on but no longer bothered me. Sergeant Battle, on the other hand, picked up where Wooten left off, keeping the harassment pressure on day in and day out. Why the two of them did this I will never know, but again, we will return to that subject in "Reflections."

On one of these pitch-black nights near the Laotian border, I had to pee. There had been no time to dig in or hooch up, just enough to roll out our poncho liners and cover up. I sat there for a minute and let my eyes adjust to the dim glow on the ground. I could make out a tree trunk here, a fern base there, and GIs causing large black spots on the ground where they lay rolled up in their liners. I knew where each man in the CP was lying, including Sergeant Battle. I pondered certain consequences as the devil took over my common sense. I stood up and walked with stealth through the ink-black night to Battle's resting place some 20 feet away. I could not figure out which was his head or feet, so I pulled out my weapon of revenge and hosed him down from one end to the other. I was nearly relieved, when he woke up and figured out what was going on, so I concentrated the remainder in the direction of the noises.

Of course, in those days I could shoot six feet away, so I figured that he would never know who it was as I slowly crept back to my own black spot, with Battle making more noise than he should, thrashing about and cursing in low tones. He crawled about the CP, finding others and interrogating them as to his misfortune. Soon enough, I could hear and actually see his path of travel in my direction! I lay silent until his groping in the darkness finally located my spot. He grabbed and shook my liner and in a low growl said, "Flory, did you piss on me?" Acting like I was waking up, I said, "Oh-oh-shit, I'm awake—I'm awake. Is it my watch? Where's the radio?" He repeated, "Doc, did you piss on me?" I said, "What?!" He said, "Forget it" and continued his mission hunting for others, until a crisp low report was heard from the platoon leader, "Battle, cease and desist now!"

Within a few weeks, Sergeant Battle, D.A., and Wooten would be leaving the company, as they were original members of the unit, and their time was up in the field. They survived the war and went back to the "world." During that last couple of weeks, however, Battle must have had some inkling that it may have been me that hosed him that night. I got the evil eye from time to time, but he finally left me alone. (He had messed with the medic far too long.)

Chaplains were assigned to most military units. In our case, they made visits to us field troops while on firebases and sometimes on LOG days. They would form groups or talk to us as individuals. They performed various church services, such as Mass for the Catholics.

They became the closest thing we had to psychological advisers or counselors and were just plain good morale builders. One day a new chaplain showed up but played the game totally different. He was in full field gear and stayed with us for weeks in the bush. He rotated from platoon to platoon and from company to company. He was an extremely gung-ho airborne trooper who carried a Bible as he humped the jungle. He went with recons, with dog handlers, and he walked with the point men on a regular basis. Chaplain Corbin Cherry was a captain, and he was a terrific morale builder whenever it was our turn to share him.

Chaplin Cherry did not carry a gun unless it came from a cache of enemy weapons. He conducted himself no differently than any other grunt and shared the extra loads of C4, belts of M-60 ammo, or whatever. He was always first on the scene, assisting the medics with the dead and the wounded. He was a very intelligent, motivated, and clever counselor who was on a never-ending quest of reminding us of our origin and responsibility to our Maker. He was a jokester, a prankster, fun to be around, a person you do not forget. I recognized him immediately when he showed up at our 2005 reunion at the dude ranch in Tulsa, Oklahoma.

By late January or early February 1969, I had been in-country nearly half of my tour. I was living life as a hardened infantry soldier, and 95 percent of the day-to-day talk was of military matters, from the flavor of your last C rat to the last mission, the next mission, or the whereabouts of the platoons or sister companies. We didn't forget about our civilian world; it was just more like a dream. Then a letter from home would arrive, oh those precious letters. My family and extended family did a wonderful job of keeping a steady flow of letters and the occasional care package coming my way. They were fun letters, funny letters, informational, of concern, good news or bad. My sister, June, then a senior, explained how "dead" it was in the halls of the school now that the class of '67 was gone. Mom always included a quote from the scriptures or a pamphlet from her church (mentoring her black sheep son). Mother did the writing for Dad, as he just didn't care to write much and probably didn't pen more than 20 words during my 730 days in the service. Mom wrote about everything, including the exploits of my dad, who had started construction on a full-sized pontoon boat, along with his week-by-week progress, including pictures. My cousin Bob Flory's wife, Joey, wrote to me and Cousin Bill on a continual basis. Bob had purchased an old cable crane, and I read of the blow-by-blow action as he restored it to working order, including a new paint job. He began earning extra money digging irrigation ponds for local farmers, and he is still digging holes. There were a few old girlfriends who corresponded, along with other classmates stationed in Vietnam. I was told that Jim Sowa, class of '66, was stationed near Da Nang. I got his address, but the very next letter announced that he had been killed by the rotor of a helicopter while volunteering to unload wounded men from a medevac at the field hospital. A sudden gust of wind tipped the helicopter sideways as he and others carried the letters away from the LZ.

I also received care packages from women and men with familiar names who were involved with the VFW back home. Words of encouragement came from veterans of previous wars. I kept a notepad in the liner of my helmet and used it constantly to record notes for my next opportunity to write letters home. It was unfortunate, but for most "packs," 95 percent of the letters and photos we received needed to be destroyed shortly after receiving them. It was impossible to pack very much of that sort of thing and no way to get it to the rear.

Another mission ended and we flew to a defensive guard position called Pohl Bridge.

Third platoon pulled guard duty at Pohl Bridge on two occasions during my time with B Company. It was good duty and always hard to leave when it was time to return to the jungle. The bridge was quite new, built by US Army engineers, and it crossed the Perfume River just southwest of Hue, between Firebases Birmingham and Camp Eagle. It was built on steel pipes at least 16 inches in diameter that were driven into the riverbed to support the flat wooden deck that went some 300 to 350 feet across. The deck of the bridge was probably some 20 feet above the natural waterline, wide enough and strong enough to easily drive a tank across. Bridge traffic was primarily military, but civilians used it as well. The bridge provided access to Route #547, the road that traveled past our firebases and headed west into the highlands, eventually connecting to the Ashau Valley, in the Thua Thien Province.

A Navy CB (construction battalion) contingent operated a large water purification unit at the southeast side of the bridge, with their bunkers built from the very edge of the river to the edge of the road some 30 feet away. A road followed the river and intersected with the bridge road just a hundred feet to the east of the CB's station. The remaining three corners were filled with bunkers, and, in the evening, wire fences were pulled across the road at the bunker perimeter line. They opened again every morning by 0700 hours to allow the mine-sweeping trucks and crew to pass on their way west. If l recall, with the help of the CBs it took two platoons to guard the bridge and the CP was on the west end. Four of us in the CP shared one of two command bunkers, which were fairly roomy and of stud and plywood wall construction. They were buried about halfway into the ground, the upper half being completely sandbag covered. Ours had a guard's bunker built on top for night watch, and the main room had a gunport about a foot high and four feet wide just above ground level and facing the river. Standing position would be required to use the portal. The opening did add some daylight and fresh air, which helped reduce the foul swampy smell that came from the soggy dirt that was under the loose-board floor.

On our first night in the bunker, all went well until about 1200 hours when a really weird screeching noise began echoing through the bunker every few minutes. "What the heck was that?" "Don't know." A minute later, "Screechfpfpfp" again. "There is definitely something weird in this bunker with us." "Yeah, we better try to find out what it is." Out came the flashlights and we looked in and under everything but couldn't find the source of the noise. Whatever it was kept us up most of the night. I do not sleep well anyway and vowed I would find the culprit the next day. There were four bunks framed from two-by-fours and plywood on one of the bunker walls, and the bottom bunks were only a few inches above the clapboard floor covering the mud. I went on a vendetta the next day to discover what had been making the noise and pulled out anything that would come loose and took it outside. I nearly depleted the flashlight batteries before finally spotting the culprit far back in a dark corner under a bottom bunk. It was a "cricket," a really "big cricket," probably three inches long. You could troll for muskies back home with a bug like that. It was just out of reach, and I needed to remove some floorboards and dig out under the bunk to reach it. In the process I discovered the bunker had a plywood floor under about six inches of half-dried mud but did not let that distract me from my mission of capturing the noisemaker. It was only a small trick to catch him, as he had only one rear leg. He could catapult himself a good distance, but he had no control of which direction he wanted to go. I lodged him in a poly bag and showed the guys our nemesis. He was blond color, old looking, his one missing leg probably the result of previous less fortunate occupants of the bunker.

The next day Dan and I found a five-gallon pail and spent eight to 10 hours nonstop removing all the mud from the bunker and reinstalling the fine furniture (ha). The next day the floor was dry, and the smell was better. We relaxed and swam in the Perfume River, which we did every chance we had. I made good friends with the CBs by helping them fix up a very old and rusty .45-caliber "grease gun." My payment was the opportunity to shoot it into the river when it was finally operational. They really were good guys, but on one visit to their bunker, the cricket somehow slipped out of my pocket and into the dark corners of their hooch. "Oh damn," the medic messed with them just a little. While doing the gunsmithing for the CBs, I met a young girl about nine years old. Her name was Hoha, and she had a fair command of English. I knew a few Vietnamese words along with established French slang, so we communicated really well. She was very smart or streetwise and made money by selling blocks of ice to GIs. Where she got the ice, I don't know. She would take me to her parents' house in the evening. I would bring them sundries and candy bars, and Hoha would interpret as we asked each other questions.

    They were wonderful people, but so poor. Their house was typical of any along the river road. It was maybe 20 feet long by 16 feet wide, and made of poles, with a thatched roof and corrugated tin tied to the walls and no door to close the entrance. The floor was dirt, but everything was neat and tidy as possible. It was about 50 yards from the CB perimeter, so I could stay there until dark. Step through the door and there was a large wooden table to the right. The legs were sawed off, so the table was only 16 inches high. On the opposite side were two beds built of tightly stretched woven reeds, six feet by six feet, 20 inches off the floor and attached directly to the walls with a woven partition between them. They were like wicker, stretched as tight as a trampoline. Wicker shelves above held a few blankets and a meager supply of clothing. To the far right a partition divided the house from the cooking area. The kitchen was the width of the house and five feet wide with no tables or counters. Aluminum and porcelain pots and pans hung from the walls. A dirt-and-stone hearth in one corner with a cast-iron tripod above hot coals held a cast-iron kettle, 20 inches in diameter. Bundles of willow switches hung from the round pole rafters, ready to become fuel for cooking. The opposite side contained wicker shelves with tin cans and bags holding whatever. There was no refrigeration and no electricity, only candles for light at night. When "mama-san" cooked, she propped a stick under a tin flap just behind the hearth to create a draft and keep the house (hut) from filling with smoke.

    Hoha invited me to her house in the evening a time or two. Their neighbors would come over and all of them stepped up onto the table, formed a circle, assumed the "kimchi squat" (sit like a dog) position, and played card games for hours. They held cards in their hands and between their toes, chatted quietly, briskly, and happily between themselves, paying little attention to me as I sat on the corner of the table, as there were no chairs in the house.

    In turn, Hoha and several kids were allowed inside the military perimeter. She would find me, sit down beside me, and crack betel nut seeds and feed me the meats. They were very good, somewhat like sunflower seeds.

Some older Vietnamese women chewed betel nut leaves, and, in time, their teeth would turn red and eventually a glossy jet black. They loved to smile at everyone, showing them off.

One day an old woman came up the street, an "idiot stick" (GI slang for shoulder pole) over her shoulder, suspending heavy articles fore and aft, and leaving behind a trail of smoke. Hoha said, "Would you like to have lunch?" The old mama-san was a traveling restaurant. Hoha flagged her to the side of the road, and the lady set her wares on a level spot, then laid the shoulder pole to the side. The rear portion had a hardened clay hearth with an area molded in to fit a small kettle and teapot over a bed of hot coals. It also supported other pans and utensils. The front portion contained the dishes and cups, along with a supply of vegetables, fruit, seasoning, and extra water. We had a nice pork-based soup, a salad topped off with orange slices, and hot tea. I paid the lady what Hoha suggested, plus a tip, and she was on her way. I estimated that the weight of the mobile restaurant was equal, or more, to the weight of the woman.

Back in our bunker, we awoke one night to intense gunfire on the opposite side of the bridge. We bailed out of our sacks and looked through the gunport for answers. A Quad-50 machine gun mounted on the back of a deuce-and-a-half was parked near the water. It had a spotlight mounted to it, and we could see the shadowed side of a sampan floating down the river toward the bridge. The men had been ordered to destroy it, fearing it could be loaded with explosives. The .50-caliber is an impressive gun as it is, but when you mount four of them together on a turret and crank up all four guns fully automatic, you do not want to be on the business end. The sampan was shredded to pieces in less than a minute, as tracers could be seen hitting the bridge pilings. The excitement was over, and we went back to our bunks, as tomorrow we would be making an assault on the next mission. This one had a name; I believe it was called "Operation Jeb Stewart." I believe that all of our missions at this point took us on one side or the other of the Ashau, as we prodded farther north on each new assault. The terrain was getting rougher, and good LZs were harder to find. A couple of times the choppers could get in close to an open spot, but the ground was too steep to land. The pilot would hover as close as possible while we jumped to the ground. This is a dangerous time for the pilots because sudden weight loss affects the controls of the craft. We would take our primary rucksacks off, stand out on the landing rails, and, at the signal from a door gunner, drop our packs to the ground, then jump off. Poor old Danny failed to get the instructions on our first jump of this kind and bailed out with his ruck on his back. His legs held up just fine, but something tore loose in his shoulder. He needed a couple of Darvon painkillers that night, and he complained about that shoulder the remainder of his tour.

On one of these missions, we were once again assigned dog handlers, and like our chaplains, they rotated from platoon to platoon and company to company. This time it was two dogs and handlers. Again, these guys were brave men and worked the point. The company was split into the three platoons as usual, and we were working different approaches to a hill. The dog team was with 1st or 2nd Platoon and making recon up a steep path. At some point, the dogs detected something ahead, but it was too late. The NVA ambush killed both handlers and one of the dogs.

We (YD Platoon) were several hundred yards away and, of course, went into code red alert. When we heard shots fired, we began guarding the flanks. As the platoon in contact started trading volleys of gunfire with the enemy, we began to move in their direction. In due time we joined up with their platoon. The ambush and firefight were over with, and we aided with the aftermath. There were no immediate LZs available, and the KIAs needed to be carried on makeshift litters through tough terrain. If I recall, it took more than 24 hours to get the two dead men to a place where their bodies could be choppered back to the rear. Tasks like that are dreaded, and nearly every man takes his turn carrying the bodies. Revenge may have come later, while making an NDP on a very high and steep-sided ridge. The platoon was dug in, night had just fallen, and a few of us in the CP were chatting quietly. At the spot where we stopped, the sky was open to the east because of an old landslide that took a 100-foot swath of jungle down the side of the ridge. The sky was like a giant movie screen full of stars and we saw the outline of nearby hills with just enough light to see some detailed terrain. The view was beautiful, and we were, most likely, enjoying a clear sky, when suddenly we saw a flash of light and a spark trail streak into the sky, arc to the southwest, and disappear. "Wow! What the hell was that? Rocket—it must be a rocket." Then came another. "Holy shit, it's got to be gooks shooting at Da Nang or Camp Eagle." Captain Pierce T. Graney, our company commander at the time, jumped on the radio and began calling in warnings to those areas. "Wow!" Number three just went off and our red leg (slang for artillery forward observer) had his map laid out, locating our position and orienting the map to the terrain. He said, "Keep an eye peeled on that spot, then we will locate it on the map. I will direct artillery to the area and walk it in." Captain Graney was busy on the radio, trying to find out if there were any friendlies in that area, and the answer was no. By then two or three more rockets had launched, and we had the spot marked quite well on the map. The red leg could have been Bill (Tiny) Koffman, I no longer remember, but he was very good! The first round from the artillery looked like a perfect hit, then the red leg ordered the gun battery to "Fire for effect!" They pumped 15 or 20 big ones in and blew up everything on the side of that hill.

A Marine unit close enough to the vicinity was directed to scout the target the next day. We learned later that it was a good strike, and that guns, rocket launchers, equipment, and bodies were found. Lord have pity on the NVA soldiers who were trying to rocket one of our bases. If there were any survivors, they are probably still wondering how anyone knew their hiding place. We never found out where the rockets landed; however, it was more dangerous now, and more caution needed to be used as we set out each day to do our job. We were on another ridge, not unlike the one just described, inching along a trail that followed the razorback. Many of the point men truly seemed to have a natural instinct for discerning trouble. As we came to a saddle in the ridge that was 150–200 feet across, with an open sight line straight through, we thought, "What a spot for an ambush." It was midday, hot as usual, and the point man took great caution making his way down the saddle and up the opposite side to reconnect with the ridge. David Krautscheid told the story, as he was the point slack man (next behind point or last man in a group or last squad in a company, etc.) that day. When the point crested the saddle, he spotted an NVA lying on the ground off to the side of the trail behind a bush. He froze for an instant, then realized the perpetrator of what could have been a very successful ambush was sleeping!

The point man took aim and shot the NVA where he lay with his RPG launcher in hand. At that moment, a second NVA stood up quickly between the trunk of a split tree, but before he could collect himself from the surprise, the point man once again responded with his M-16, and the two NVA both lay silent. We searched them for papers and collected their weapons, which always made an additional burden for someone (that includes the medics). We were never immune to packing extra M-60 ammunition, an ax, Charlie-4 (composition-4, plastic explosive), det cord (clear plastic tubing filled with composition-4), or weapons collected from the enemy. It also seemed to be an unwritten necessity for the medic to have a look at the bodies, "the coroner effect." But from their wounds, anyone could deduce a zero survival.

We proceeded down that ridge for some distance, then made our way back the same route to the NDP from the previous night. On the way back, trip wires were set up coming and going on the trail from the location of the bodies, and the red leg marked the coordinates of the spot. Sure enough, late that night the booby trap was tripped. The red leg had already called the coordinates into the nearest artillery battery, and the deadly 105-howitzer rounds pounded that spot hard.

One of the jobs I feared the most was night ambush. There were various reasons for using them, but typically they were used when the company was in full force. We would rendezvous at an NDP spot, then send out a five- or six-man squad back down the way we had come in. We moved to a predetermined location, got off the trail just before it was too dark to see, and guarded the trail. The idea was to give early warning to the larger group if enemy were sneaking up. These were times when you rarely slept at all, you didn't make shelters, no digging in, and there were no ponchos. You didn't dare try to feel at home. I accompanied these ambush squads 10 or 12 times during my tour. The company as a whole was at less risk if one medic was lost, and I was always an extra gun on the ambush until someone needed me.

It rained on many nights, but on one occasion while on ambush, we were in a small hole in the earth. A very large vine encircled the hole several times. I was able to take comfort in the wee hours of the morning while bridged between the loops of the vine. The rain became very intense and eventually filled the pit. There was no choice but for all of us to stay there, half-submerged, until there was enough morning light to safely join the company. It's hard to describe just how miserable you can feel. One thing about the 101st (maybe all field units) is that you are required to be "standing tall" (as possible under the conditions) every day. We would be in the field for 10 or 15 days, half of them raining, humping six–10 kilometers per day up and down mountains, sweating and stinking badly in the 100-degree-plus steaming jungle. After sleeping and crawling on the jungle floor, in the same uniform you started with, you were filthy and had a brackish odor. But, by golly, you needed to shave every other day, no matter what.

Once again, you just did not pack anything you did not need. Guys would form coalitions of three men. One packed a mirror, one packed the aerosol shave cream, and the third packed the razor. Now keep in mind, water was often rationed if it hadn't rained, or you couldn't get any morning dew off your poncho. If shaving was required during that time, we would first each pour a little water in the cap from the aerosol can, then use some method of drawing lots for who got to use water first, second, then third. The shave cream went on a dry face. You let it soak in for a minute, shave a swath, and spin the razor in the cap to clean it. By the time the cap got to the third man, well, we won't go there. The real airborne dudes (jump-qualified) always said that it was much easier to pound the whiskers in with their gun butt and bite them off from the inside!

The AO (area of operation) we were in during the early months of 1969 was fairly active with enemy. It may be hard to think about it this way, but we could take solace in knowing that if something moved in front of you, just shoot it. There were Montagnard (native aborigines) people out there, but they always knew where we were and stayed away. It was NVA soldiers, American soldiers, and jungle animals, period. Things were much tougher for the troops in the lowlands, where there were farmers, villagers, kids, Vietcong, and NVA that looked and dressed like everyone else. Where we were, there were only NVA, and most wore khaki shirts and shorts.

So anyway, one day we were inching our way up some ridge and took an abrupt turn down into a deep draw. It took nearly half the morning to reach the bottom. By midafternoon we were getting back close to the summit on the opposite side. We were moving through the jungle, but not on any established trail. Reconning for hours on end is tedious work for everyone, not just the point man. Silence is truly golden, and hand signals are used a great deal of the time. Up ahead a right arm goes out slowly, forearm vertical, fist clinches, then opens again, and waves left, then right behind you someone else picks up on the signal and repeats the command, and so on it goes down the string of men that are 20–30 feet apart. The men sink low, ease 10–20 feet off to the side, seek cover if they can, but watching the flanks carefully, quietly, and the line of men nearly disappears. Time passes slowly as the points probe forward into the unknown until they are satisfied. Then the remainder of the men can safely move forward.

The "slack man" bringing up the rear of the column has a very tough job as well. He not only needs to watch where he is going and watch his flank, he needs to study the terrain as it moves away, making sure no one is following.

The best "slack men" always seemed to be short guys, and they loved to carry a single-shot M-79 grenade launcher. They kept a buckshot (beehive) round chambered and an M-79 grenade round in the other hand, at the ready. Meanwhile, I had no idea how close we were to the summit, and, for whatever reason, I was about the sixth man back from the point. Usually I ended up around 16th–18th in a platoon of 28 to 30 men. We were moving forward (and upward) at a steady pace for a while, and the usual signal to sit tight and watch the flanks came through the line. I moved off to the right this time and sat down 15 to 20 feet off the projected line of travel. It was a nice quiet day under the triple canopy that was letting in just a little more light than usual. Time passed, and I noticed a rather large bat flying through the second layer of trees and taking a perch upside down on a limb some 75 degrees up from my horizontal sight line. I was looking at it, thinking, "Oh that's a big sucker, nothing like that in Michigan."

As my head was cocked back, I noticed movement closer to me. I was sitting on the ground, under a giant fern, my feet pointed down the slope. Some of the ferns are huge in the rainforest, with six or eight branches jutting out from a single stump, a single leaf fixed to the rhubarb-like stalk, some four to six feet in diameter. I looked up slightly higher at the connection of the leaf and stalk, and there was a brilliant green bamboo viper, his head and the first 12 inches of his body hanging straight down, looking directly at me and sticking his tongue out. "Oh crap." I am sitting there, the butt of my M-16 between my legs and already pointing straight up. I moved the barrel directly in line with the snake and thought about pulling the trigger. Heck, we weren't on any kind of a trail. Maybe no enemy would hear the gun's report and mark our position. Well, on second thought, I decided I can't take a chance on that. Even if everything was fine, I'd be in big trouble with everyone, including the platoon leader. I chose to move five feet closer to the line of travel, and catching the attention of a few men around me, pointed to the viper's location.

The signal to move forward came once again, and we progressed forward (and up) for another 15 or 20 minutes. I was looking up through the men as we were catching up to Sergeant Wayne Carrara, from New York, who was first man out on point. It looked like we were reaching the top, when Carrara, while stepping over a log, stumbled, caught himself on a tree, swung partly around the tree before stopping, and yelled at the top of his lungs, "Gooks! Gooks!" He righted himself, stepped back in shock, tripped backward over the log he just went over, and cartwheeled backward down the slope toward us. Sure as shit, two gooks who were sleeping on a thatch bunk jumped up, racked shells into their AK-47s, and started spraying the area with bullets. All of us dove to the ground, seeking the nearest tree, and swung into position to return fire. The NVA definitely had the upper hand for the first clip of ammunition. There were red tracers headed uphill from every direction, green tracers headed downhill from every direction, and, despite the noise of all the automatic weapons, I could hear the bolts of the AKs slapping shut in rapid action. The volley quit as abruptly as it started. A signal to fall back was given, and I hunted for casualties but found none! Lordy momma, that was a tad too close. Later on, I took a bit of an ass-chewing from our platoon leader, Lieutenant Pue, for being too close to point.

We hustled back down the hill a short distance and formed into a DP as Lieutenant Pue called in gunships. I'm not sure how the birds marked the target, other than the prominence of the hill, but Pue placed them correctly over the target. They must have been sitting ready to take off or already in flight, because it was only minutes before they arrived and begun pouring "piss and shit" all over that ridge, with rockets blasting, the rumbling *blatttttt* of mini-guns, then more rockets (the sound of a mini-gun firing at a rate of thousands of rounds per minute reminded me of foghorns on the big ore boats making their way on the St. Marys River back in the UP of Michigan).

The gunships approached almost always from behind us, flying at high speed, passing our position, then pouring their ordnance into the jungle, taking turns circling around, and doing it again several times until their weapons were empty. We got a glimpse of the birds as they maneuvered above. They were Cobra gunships and had such incredible firepower that if anyone was in this field of fire, they were in big trouble. Our enemies knew it and usually didn't stick around long. When the Cobras finished their work of chewing up the hilltop, it was our turn once again to head to the top. We moved in quickly as the birds were leaving, hoping that if any unfriendlies were remaining that their heads would still be down.

Upon reaching the summit, we found two things right away. One was a trail unlike anything we had ever encountered previously. It was three to five feet wide and packed down hard from foot travel. As we explored the trail later, we found that the enemy had created steps in the steep areas and made improvements of other sorts to allow foot soldiers, their equipment, and supplies to move quickly through the forest. At the spot where Sergeant Carrara tripped, there was a nice two-man thatch bunk with a thatch roof bridged between two trees, and it was all well used. More interesting, however, were hand-hewn rungs lashed with vines and bamboo to one of the two trees. The tree was quite large and leaned out over the edge of the hilltop. It went out through the canopy to a perch, and from that point the NVA could watch for aircraft. That spot was the pinnacle of a ridge coming along in one direction. At the high point, the ridge and the trail took a sharp turn and began descending again. This seemed the Holy Grail of trails, and we were all amazed by the sight of it. We now knew the location of a serious supply route, which was good, but on the other hand, the NVA were not going to be happy we knew about it. We were guaranteed to find enemy if we stuck to this path long enough. The CP stayed close to the lookout tree as the platoons split up to recon a distance down both directions of the trail. Meanwhile, I had time to study the effects of mini-gun and rocket fire while the aroma of the explosives was still in the air. A rocket trajectory was limited to the direct flight of the gunship, but the pilots could direct the warbirds about any way they wished. The mini-gun, however, is turret-mounted and could be rotated left or right, up or down.

The jungle, for the most part, was unaffected, but upon closer observation there were shards of iron frag, plastic, steel, and aluminum everywhere. It was surprising how many bullet holes could be found in everything. It would have been a very unhealthy place to be when the Cobras were in action. It seemed that no one was around, but after about 20 minutes, shots rang out down one direction of the trail. Then came a short volley, followed by silence. A radio report documented one enemy body. As related by the point man, this was one time that the NVA dress code didn't apply. The gook stepped out into the trail, his AK at the ready, wearing a blue Mickey Mouse sweatshirt. The gook didn't know he was stepping out in front of "Snake," a man who had grown up as a very successful hunter in the backwoods of Minnesota, and he was a very experienced point man. The gook died from lead poisoning. (Dan told me recently that this event was November 25, 1968, at 3:15 in the afternoon.) That night, sleep came hard, as we knew this was Charlie's backyard, and the tension was high. As I tried to sleep, my mind drifted back to the viper and how terrible the day might have been if I had pulled the trigger, alerting the two NVA lookouts that we were coming.

Weeks had passed by now, and it was time to go back to a firebase. We found a good site for an LZ on a very high razorback ridge. Again, it was an area where the land had collapsed from the side of the steep ridge, carrying everything down the side of the hill and creating a huge, very steep washout and leaving the ridge open on one side. All we had to do was open up the other side, a great idea, and a great spot. But there were very old, very large trees in the proposed LZ that were four feet in diameter and over 100 feet tall. Well, we couldn't chop or saw them down, so out came the C-4. We had rendezvoused with a sister company at this spot, so there was plenty of the explosive. It would have been difficult for the enemy to assault our position other than from the top of the ridge. The sister company guarded one direction and we the other, with the proposed LZ in the center. The axes stayed busy on the smaller trees, as some of us performed as demolition "experts." A few days earlier one of our guys found nearly a bushel of Polish dynamite in a hollow tree. Yes, that's right, Polish dynamite. It was cold and wet, but we packed it along anyway.

What the hay, why not use up this old dynamite too? So, we held a wad of Polish dynamite sticks against a tree trunk, placed two or three bars of Charlie-4 against it, wrapped demolition cord tightly around the tree, shoved a blasting cap in the end of the det cord, strung a detonator wire as far away as possible, and touched her off. This needed to be repeated several times on two of the trees to blow them in half. Eventually a treeless gap through the ridge appeared. The last tree that went down fell across the high point of the washed-out landslide, blocking some of the approach. It had one large limb sticking straight out from the trunk and into the proposed flight way. We called in a Huey to test the opening, and the answer was "negative." The limb had to go. "Snake, Doc [we had a reputation by then], get that limb off there." Dan shimmied up first with me right behind toting the ax. Dan worked his way into position, wrapped his legs around the trunk like riding an old bull, and tried to make good swings at the 16-inch-diameter limb. Dan was no quitter, and I did whatever I could to brace his position. But through prior experience, both of us quickly came to the conclusion that the limb would not yield to this approach. "Screw it, blow the sucker!" We shimmied back down the trunk, which was at least 40 feet above the crevasse, and falling off would have been very bad. We climbed up the trunk, this time with me in the lead. Dan packed three bars of C-4 and det cord. I placed them around the crotch of the limb, held them in place with det cord, shoved in the blasting cap, and we shimmied down the trunk. The view, by the way, was quite spectacular from the height of the leaning tree. It would have been nice to stay for a while and look around.

The demolition was successful, and the limb came crashing down and tumbled nearly to the bottom of the crevasse. Another chopper was summoned to retest the LZ and was en route as men walked back and forth through the gap in the ridge that probably looked like a reverse Mohawk haircut from the air. Bang, a shot rang out from far below in the washout.

At this stage of the game in our on-the-job training, at least 95 percent of us could tell without question the difference between an AK-47 report and an M-16. In about the time it took to make that distinction, I was already diving for the dirt and hollering "Sniper!" I swear it wasn't five seconds before someone on the opposite side of the gap was shouting "Medic! Medic!" Visions of Jimmy Green raced through my head as I scrambled for my aid bag. "Was that sniper waiting for a new shithead to go prancing across the gap?" I thought. Carrying my ruck in one hand and with a 15-yard head start, I breached the opening like a sprinter on speed, reached the other side, and skidded to a stop like a baseball player at home plate. There the guy was, just five feet away, with another head wound! But this guy was acting just fine. I began to work on him and found that the bullet had carved a path through the tissue of his scalp about three inches long, a half inch wide, and a quarter inch deep, with his skull almost visible. It was as if you used a large round rat-tail file and ground this kerf into his head. The wound was hardly bleeding, but I cleaned it and applied a compress. The only way to hold it on was to wrap an Ace bandage around his head, under his chin, and so on. He looked a bit like a mummy, but trust me, he knew just how close he came to having no head at all. For whatever reason, the sniper didn't harass us anymore that day. He probably knew we could have made it rain lead into the trees at the base of the washout.

The chopper arrived the second time and made a careful approach. This time there was enough room, but barely. Hats off once again for the pilots and crews of those helicopters. If it could be done, they would do it. Keep in mind, the jungle floor had been undisturbed for hundreds or even thousands of years in this remote place. When that first bird took off with the wounded man and five other GIs, the rotor wash sent everything that was lying loose sailing into the bush on either side. I stood behind a large tree for cover and as the chopper made its exit, I felt a terrible burning

Transition to Duty by Leo Flory.

sensation at the top of my right boot. "Good Lordy, Momma," it got worse very quickly, and I realized something was biting me! I stomped my foot down repeatedly until, voila, a centipede about the size of an Old Dutchman cigar hit the ground. He was using all of his hundred legs to make an escape when my leg, now on automatic pilot, came down again and turned him into yellow goo. I don't know what toxins are in those bugs, but I do know I spent the next 45 minutes reeling in pain, my leg half-paralyzed. Yet today, I can still find the scars of the two holes where that thing sank his fangs at the very top of my boot, through my Army-issue socks and just below the taut blousing string of my jungle fatigues.

It was always good to leave the jungle. But this time there was a little added anticipation in the air as the brass said we were taking an "in-country R&R" at a place called Culco Beach.

I can't recall if sister companies were replacing us or not, but as we boarded the helicopter and sand flew precariously out of that dangerously narrow LZ, I was just glad to go. We flew to a firebase, where we boarded deuce-and-a-halves once again and headed for the east coast, this time just south of Hue City. Highway One appeared to be in very well-maintained condition, widened and raised (huh?), a nice ride. It was also bustling with people, ox carts, mopeds, motorcycles, cars, and bicycles as our convoy made its way to the port village on the Gulf of Tonkin.

For the complete story of Leo Flory, contact him at:
P.O. Box 338, Decatur, MI 49045; (269) 423–8115; floryenterprise@gmail.com.

Five

SP-5 William "Neil" Keddie, Jr., Camp Eagle, I Corps, 1969–70

HHC 1st, 502nd, 101st Airborne Division E Company Recon

Combat Medical Badge, Vietnam Campaign Medal, Bronze Star, Meritorious Service, Army Commendation Medal, Good Conduct Medal

In 1969 I flunked out of college. I went back home to Dallas, Texas, where I grew up and lived with my parents. I went to work at a local hospital. My mother and my sister were both nurses, so we had a history of the medical field in our family. One day in April I came home from work and I peeped in the mailbox. I didn't have a key to get in it, but I saw what I suspected was a draft notice. I went and got in the pool and was swimming when my mom got home. Pretty soon she came out to the pool and held up a letter and started making the trumpet sound of reveille. I knew then that it was my draft notice.

I went down to the Army recruiting office and took a test I really didn't want to pass, but I did. I went for a physical and, as always, there was one who stood out in the group. The doctor told us to bend over and grab our cheeks and spread them. One guy bent over and grabbed his mouth cheeks and the doctor had to explain to him to spread his butt cheeks. Anyway, I passed the physical. I was lucky they had already picked all the guys they were getting for the Marines, so I went to the Army. My date of induction was June 23, 1969.

We took a bus ride that took all day and arrived at the base. I'm not going through basic except to say I didn't care for it. Except to say that the exercise was horrible because in July it was 110 degrees and we had to exercise on asphalt several times and when we did push-ups we all ended up with burnt hands. We had all kinds of tests we had to take. We were asked if we had ever committed a crime, and of course I put no. But then the test went on, like how do you spell *murder* and how do you spell *auto theft* and on and on. I always thought that was strange. After the test they gave us what was called a dream sheet, which asked us what we wanted to do in the Army. I said I wanted to do something medical. They said how about a medical technician, and I agreed to that. We finished basic training and the day of graduation the drill instructor said you have finished the easy part except for those of you going to Fort Meade. You will have it easy there. The next day we got on a bus and went to Fort Sam Houston. We got there and I thought this was going to be wonderful. I'm going to Fort Sam and I'm going to medical school. This is exactly what I asked for on the dream sheet.

I'm in combat medical school to be a medic. The training was more the type for what happened in Korea instead of Vietnam. We had a drill where a four-man team had to carry a stretcher through an obstacle course. That was more what they did in a situation in Korea. If you were in the jungle in Vietnam, there was no way you were going to be able to carry a stretcher through the jungle.

Other things they taught us were how to put up tents and all, also things that seemed more like what they did in Korea instead of Vietnam.

P-5 Neil Keddie's first full day in-country for the 101st. He had just completed his paperwork for the 101st and was sitting on a bunker when a fire mission began.

We had a time that we were going to go out for an exercise and we were going to be ambushed. They took us out on this truck, and I was assigned as a guard. I was looking for signs of an ambush and I was supposed to report when I saw anything. It was muddy in the area where we went, and I could see tracks of other trucks and areas where they had stopped and turned around, so as soon as we got up there, I yelled "Ambush!" and we all jumped off the truck. The drill sergeant asked where it was, and I said I didn't know but this was obviously where it was going to be because this was where the truck turned around. We walked a few feet and we got ambushed. The point is that what we trained for wasn't going to apply in Vietnam.

In November 1969, after graduating from medical school, I got my orders to Vietnam. I went home for 30 days' leave and then reported to San Francisco. The closer it got to actually going to Vietnam, the more scared

His second day in Vietnam there was a B-52 bombing 30 miles from SP-5 Neil Keddie (standing). It made the bunks rock back and forth as if they were in an earthquake. Other soldiers unknown.

I got. I remember lying in a bunk one night and there was light coming through a window and I could see several empty bunks. I wondered how many guys had lain on these bunks that went to Vietnam and never came home.

The next day we caught a plane from Travis Air Force Base. We stopped in Hawaii to refuel and then we went to Wake Island. It was weird when we landed there because I knew there had been a major battle there in World War II and all it looked like was a sand dune. I wondered, my God, how many people died for this little piece of ground? Then we flew over Iwo Jima and it looked like nothing but a little pimple in the ocean. I again wondered how many thousands died on that island. We later landed in the Philippines and were there for about four hours. We finally reached Vietnam late at night.

As a medic I had no idea what I was getting into. After we landed, I went through some processing and then flew to Ben. We had all medics and cooks on board. When we got ready to land, there were rounds going off all over the place. "Oh my God, we are being hit by artillery!" But it was actually aluminous rounds going off. When I got off the plane, the first thing that hit me was the stench. My God it was terrible. There was a line of guys that were getting ready to board a plane to go home. It was almost indescribable how they looked. Their eyes were glazed, they looked really worn, but they sure gave us crap. "There's my replacement," "Hey, cherry," things like that.

We boarded a bus that had all the windows caged so grenades couldn't be thrown in. They drove us to the headquarters, and I got my orders to the 101st Airborne. I thought I'm not qualified for airborne. Then the rumor started that they would give us a crash course in how to jump from a plane, which freaked me out, but it was just a rumor. There was no crash course for us. We spent the night at the base and there was a B-52 raid about 30 miles north of us. When they dropped their bombs, the ground around us just shook. The bunks were rocking back and forth. It looked like we were having an earthquake.

The next day we went through preparation training with the M-16 and the M-69. We were all cooks and medics and had never seen these weapons before, much less shot any of them. It was a lot of fun. They had moved us around to couple of different places for the P training and then we were going to go to the 101st. They put us on a plane and flew us up to Camp Evan. The airstrip was too short for landings, and they had to stop really quick. One of the guys sitting beside me threw up in his steel helmet. It was a quick landing on a fast stop. We got off the plane and went through processing. The first thing I got assigned to was trash detail. We had to go around, pick up the trash, and take it to this big dump area. We were on the back of the trucks and got to the dump. There were villagers standing at the dump when we pulled up. They just swamped the trucks and took all the garbage off the trucks and left with it. We didn't have to do a thing. They took it all. It was very sad to me.

We finished up P training and I was sent to headquarters battalion of the 101st at Camp Sally. I was told I was being assigned to the Recon Platoon and that's where I would be doing the rest of my tour. When I reported I found out that the senior medic was from Texas and that about a third of the recon platoon was also from Texas. I spent a lot of time talking to the other medics about what to take when we went in the field. How many supplies, should I take my rucksack, and that type of thing.

Then we got ready for what was my first mission. We went out to what was called the Salad Bowl. The Salad Bowl was kind of a round dense valley, and it looked like it had a salad in it. I was on the helicopter for the first time, and I was sitting in the middle. Flying over it, the country, the mountainous terrain, and waterfalls were beautiful. It was hard to believe there was a war being fought here. We landed in the mountains. I had a lot of gear I was carrying, and it was hard to get off the chopper, but I finally made it. Heading into the bush was really scary for me the first time. We climbed two or three hills and the first one we went up was about 65 meters. It kicked my ass going to the top of that hill. I was carrying a heavy rucksack with a lot of things I didn't need. Some of the guys helped me carry the rucksack a ways until we got to the top. We all got a breather when we got to the top and then set up a camp where we were going to run patrols from there.

My first night out I was scared to death. I didn't know what we were going to get into or what was going to happen. We didn't know who was out there or how they would get into our camp. I did my first guard duty that night. It was so dark you couldn't see your hand in front of your face. I didn't realize that we were facing Highway 1. While I was sitting there, a tank came down the highway. I just about crapped my pants because I didn't know what it was. Then the firebases started firing all kinds of artillery, which was on all sides of us. It started raining and I was soaked. We had no contact that night, but I sure was glad to see daylight come the next morning.

We moved out on a patrol the next day into an area that we were going to search. We had a platoon sergeant that we called Sergeant Rock. He had been in the field in Vietnam for three years straight. It was his choice, and he really knew what he was doing. He was the most highly decorated soldier in Vietnam. He knew the enemy and how they thought, how they moved, and he took us under his wing to teach us all he knew. Right before we went out on the patrol, Sergeant Rock showed us the map, pointed to

Five. William "Neil" Keddie, Jr.

Sgt. Jorge Otero Barretto (front) and SP-5 Neil Keddie. The sergeant was nicknamed Rock after a comic book character.

an area, and said if we were going to get hit, this is where. We were on the patrol and got hit and it was within a foot of the area where he told us we would be hit. There was a firefight and a couple of NVA soldiers were killed.

We moved out again and about an hour later we ran into some NVA soldiers. They ran down this hill partway and hid. Sergeant Rock called artillery in on them. When you called artillery in you needed at least 100 meters between you and the spot for the artillery rounds to hit. Sergeant Rock told us to pick a tree to hide behind and we did. He called the rounds in, and numerous rounds went off. We could hear some of the flak from the rounds come through the trees. When it was over, we stepped out and Sergeant Rock had a big grin on his face. We checked it out and the NVA were dead.

We completed our mission and went back to our base camp with no more contact on that mission. Sergeant Rock had a lot of nightmares and we often let him sleep and took his guard duties for him. One night he woke up and came and got me. He said the NVA had been on our line and were turning our claymore mines around and wanted me to take a couple of guys and check it out. I am a medic of all people to ask, but we went to the line and there was nothing going on. Shortly, Sergeant Rock showed up and emptied a full M-16 magazine in an empty foxhole. Then he looked at us and said to come on and we walked back to our tents. I don't know if he had a bad dream or what, but it was a real eye-opening event.

We went on another mission, and we were up on a hill, and we ran out of supplies. We had no water and no food. We were in an area where they couldn't get anyone out to us. One of the guys had gotten a package from

SP-5 Neil Keddie (right) treating Ruben Yzaguine, his FO, who had just cut his finger on a machete. Yzaguine was Keddie's first patient.

home. He had Kool-Aid packets and passed them out to all of us. We had no water but ate the Kool-Aid and had it all over our fingers. Our fingers were all colors, but the thing is we took care of each other. We had each other's backs. We were close. If there were only two of us left, we would be willing to sit back-to-back and fight till we were gone.

In December of 1969, we went on a block-and-sweep mission in several villages. We would set up at night and then sweep through the villages during the day. We would then meet up with ARVN forces that were working for us. The ARVN forces were hard to work with because they would take lunch breaks. When it came noon, they went home to eat and then they would come back. Didn't matter what was going on. They worked an eight-hour war.

We pulled a block-and-sweep on a village and didn't come up with anything. We made our way back to a pole bridge. We were getting close to the bridge, and we had a bunch of kids that were following us wanting food or anything else we could give them. We had a soldier in our group that didn't want to be a soldier or be in Vietnam and he had a real attitude. He just turned and shot one of the kids. It was a little girl. I did everything I could to save her, but she didn't make it. I still have nightmares about that today.

After all that we finally got to the bridge in the afternoon, and they had hot chow waiting for us. It turned out to be a disaster because the chow had been sitting out for hours. Flies had infested the food. Into January we started having a lot of problems with diarrhea. We all had it and we still had to complete our mission with that problem. You would wake up and there would be a pair of nasty pants hanging in the breeze. On guard duty you had guys running by you saying, "It's just me, Doc," trying to get to the latrine. This went on for weeks and we were finally able to get some guys sent to the rear to be tested. Come to find out our food had been contaminated. There were several different kinds of the diarrhea, and I had amebic diarrhea and had to go to the hospital. I was there for 12 days and lost 30 pounds. I was 180 pounds when I got to Vietnam and by the time I left, I was 130 pounds.

I had arrived there in November and about March or April I became senior medic for the platoon. We were on this mission, and we were going down this stream and it was only about ankle-deep. We would walk along and all of a sudden, the water was up to your thigh. Then as we moved along, we noticed elephant turds on the banks. Turns out that the NVA were using elephants as pack animals. We didn't run into the NVA. When we finished the mission, we cleared an area for the choppers to come in to pick us up. While we were clearing the area, we found more elephant turds. Sergeant Rock got a bag and put some turds in it, and we took it back with

SP-5 Neil Keddie (left) and an ARVN medic north of Birmingham at the Royal Tombs outside Hue.

us. He hated the operations officer, so he took them to him. He told him we needed the turds inspected to determine if the elephants were male, female, babies, and what size their assholes were. The operations officer stood there dumbfounded as Sergeant Rock walked off.

One night we got word that there was an NVA rocket platoon that was going to rocket Camp Eagle. They got our platoon together and they were going to insert us into the area where they thought they were and have us take them out. We had to pick up our claymores that we had placed out in front of our position, so we went down. This sergeant tripped a wire on one and it exploded. It tore him up pretty bad. He had shrapnel in his leg and a compound fracture. I dressed him up as best I could, and we called in a medevac. I lied like hell to him telling him he was going to be fine and okay in a few days. They took him back to the aid station and then shipped him to Japan. A few months later one of the guys got a letter from him. He said to tell the doc he was wrong. They had taken his leg off. I wasn't surprised, but when you have someone wounded like that you have to give them all the hope you can at the time. That's what I did.

After my nine months in the field, I worked at a firebase aid station a few miles down from Camp Eagle. The firebase was located on the Perfume River. I worked with two doctors, and we took care of soldiers in the area along with going to villages and treating the villagers as best we could. We treated a lot of ringworm and malaria.

We had one medic that had come in that was supposed to be my replacement but ended up being the replacement for another medic that ended up court-martialed for some things he did. He was hard to train. He would come in with reports that this guy has the shits, or this guy has a rash on his balls. I had to teach him that he needed to use medical terms when making the reports. I explained that these medical records go with these soldiers for life. It needed to be in medical terms.

We were all 18-, 19-, and 20-year-olds and did funny stuff sometimes. We had a soldier come in one day with a rash. He said, "I need you to take care of this for me. Can you give me some of that shit I got before?" I said, "Oh, you want some shit." He said, "Yes, that shit worked really well. It's some super shit. I mean it is fantastic super shit." I said, "Oh, you don't want the shit, you want the super-fantastic shit." He says yeah. I got him some ointment and I wrote on the tag "Super-fantastic shit, apply twice a day." He was happy when he left.

I had just gotten back from R&R, and I found out that Smitty, one of our friends, had set off a Vietnamese booby trap by mistake. It had blown off both his legs and one arm. We went to the hospital to see him. It was sad to see him in the condition he was in. He was restless and nurses were trying to hold him down on the bed. He was incoherent but when I walked up to the side of the bed, he snapped out of it. He recognized me and started talking to me and we talked for a while. I always wondered how it was he just snapped out of it when I walked up. A couple of days later they sent him down to Saigon and he had kidney failure and died.

At the same time, they had the battalion commander in the hospital. When he went to the field, he always had his own private shitter taken with him. He wouldn't go in the field like the rest of us. They had gone out on this mission and got attacked by the NVA. They were using the shitter to aim in on the unit. When the rounds started coming in, he ran down the hill to try to save his shitter and got hit in both legs. Come to find out he got a Silver Star for it. What is the justice in that? He gets a Silver Star for trying to save his shitter and my friend Smitty gets his name on the wall.

When I left Vietnam in November of 1970, I was given a drop to the 17th. At that time up in I Corps where I was a monsoon struck the

SP-5 Neil Keddie sitting at right. Other soldiers unknown. Waiting on the slicks to pick them up and take them to another CA.

countryside. It was a rather severe one. A couple of days before it struck, our 91C and I went back to Camp Eagle to get some supplies. On the way back to arsenal, it was raining rather hard. As we approached the bridge that led up to the firebase, we noticed the stream was up and running over it. I had Mac get out and walk across the bridge and I followed behind him to make sure we could do it. We were successful and drove on up to the firebase. About two hours later someone stopped by the aid station and told us

SP-5 Neil Keddie in a battalion ambulance near Hue.

the bridge had just washed way. We were lucky on that one. The next day, I was scheduled to go back to Phu Bai and catch a ride to Danang to catch a flight for home. The storm was getting worse and worse, and it didn't look like I was going to be able to leave, but the battalion CO sent his Huey to pick me up. It turned out I was the last one to leave for about a week. All the roads were bad leading to the arsenal. There was no way to resupply.

When I reached Danang, it turned out that the Army in all of its wisdom had created the drop but had failed to increase the number of flights in to get us out. The base was overrun with troops ready to go home. It took me a couple of days before I finally got manifested on a flight home. I remember the day we flew out of there. As I was a medic and fearful that I would get stuck in the middle seat—which I did—I had brought along a few Valiums to make the flight bearable. I waited till the wheels were up and we all applauded, then I took my pills. I passed out and knew nothing till we reached the Philippines. We got off to stretch our legs while they refueled. Basically the two guys I shared the row with had to carry me out as I was pretty out of it. When I asked them if they had served breakfast, they said yes. I moaned that I hadn't eaten mine, which they said that I had. I had no memory of eating it. Back on the plane I passed out until almost reaching "the world." We all screamed hooray and got ready to get off and get processing over with so we could get home.

When I left Vietnam, I still had six months to go before being discharged. Before I left, as usual, they had me fill out a dream sheet. They asked me what my preference was as to where I would be stationed. I told them Fort Ord because I loved Big Sur and Monterey. When I reached Fort Lewis, I received my orders, which was to join the 702nd Medical Clearing Company at Fort Meade, Maryland. I always have figured that Fort Meade was near the Atlantic so to them a coast was a coast.

My time at Fort Meade for the most part was a waste of time. The 702nd was a company that was to be ready to be sent to anywhere there was a disaster in order to set up a hospital and treat the victims. While I was there there was a disaster in Europe, but we were never called. It was probably better that we weren't as a lot of our medical tools were missing—mostly the clamps had all been pilfered by the dopers who used them to hold their joints while they smoked them.

By this time, I was an E-5 sergeant. When I arrived at Fort Meade, it had snowed a lot and our company was quite often used for nonmedical purposes. I was put in charge of a work party to shovel the snow off the sidewalks. When we got back, the first sergeant bitched at me that he had seen me and I wasn't doing it right. Of all things. I had been helping them shovel figuring—like we did in Vietnam—that one more pair of hands would make the job go faster. But no, I was supposed to be in charge, which meant that I wasn't supposed to do any work. I was supposed to supervise. From then on, I figured if they wanted me to act like a lifer I may as well look like one and carried a clipboard with me everywhere I went.

Finally, I got a job in the clinic and was able to spend the last couple of months actually treating troops as I had been trained. One side note on this: we were near where George Wallace got shot when he was running for president. It happened that one of our doctors was the first man to reach him and did what he could to treat his wounds while waiting for the ambulance.

While I was there at Fort Meade, I fell in love with Maryland. It was 180 degrees from Dallas. There were mountains to the west, major cities in the middle, along with Chesapeake Bay and the Atlantic to the east. Unlike Texas, there were four seasons, which was amazing. I changed my mind about returning to Dallas and planned to stay in Maryland when I was discharged. I made plans to go to college and settled on Salisbury State College on the Eastern Shore of Maryland. It was only a few minutes away from the bay and 30 miles to the Atlantic and the resort town of Ocean City.

It's funny now, but not so when it happened. On Memorial Day I was returning from Salisbury, where I had been looking for a job and a place to live. I was crossing the bridge over the Severn River when suddenly four jets came over head about 100 feet above us. I was still suffering from PTSD so when they flew over the top of us, I almost drove us off the bridge. It turned out to be the Blue Angels performing for the celebration at the Naval Academy.

When I finally was discharged, I moved to Salisbury and got a job as an attendant in the ER of the local hospital. It was a great job. I was there for about six years while I went to school and for about a year after I graduated. It was great because it was helping to feed my adrenaline rush from my days as a medic. I had to laugh. One day I was taking a patient's blood pressure. The nurse supervisor asked me who taught me to take blood pressure. I answered back the US government. The nurse had no reply.

Six

SP-4 Dwayne Williams, Phu Bai, 1970–71

85th Evac Hospital

Combat Medical Badge, National Defense Medal, Vietnam Service Medal, Vietnam Campaign Medal, Rifle Expert

I was a Kennedy husband. If you don't know what a Kennedy husband is, it meant you were exempt from draft if you were married. Kennedy was killed so that changed and I became 1-A eligible for the draft. I was married and had every intention of not being drafted until that time. It wasn't long and I got drafted on July 20, 1969. For those that may not know, that was the day we set foot on the moon with Neil Armstrong.

I went to St. Louis, Missouri, for induction. We went through the physical and we stood for muster after all the exams were done—for those of us who passed all the exams. That was most of us and this guy came up and said he wanted all of us to go downstairs and out from there is a bus. "You need to get aboard. We are taking you to the airport." The Army base for basic was only halfway across Missouri and we never thought we would fly such a short distance, but that was before we found out we were going to California. There were a lot of telephone calls made and a lot of boo-hooing. It was a shock for most of us and being married and having to call was quite shocking.

Fort Ord, California, is located on Monterey Bay. I learned to hate the sand. We marched in the sand and every place we went we walked in the sand. It just wore our asses out. I was lucky to get through it. I got an upper respiratory infection and spent about a week in the hospital. When I got out, I had to go straight to the rifle range. I had been to the range only one time before but being from southern Illinois, I knew how to shoot. The rifle they gave me was already sighted in, so I didn't have any difficulty qualifying. The target was so big to me, and I ended up being the top shooter in the company and they took me to meet the colonel. He wanted to meet the guy that was the top shooter. Hell, the rest of the guys were from California, and they didn't know which end the bullet came out of. I ended up being an outstanding recruit when we graduated for my performance on the rifle range.

The night before we shipped out, everyone was going to go their separate ways and we all ended up getting drunk. For some reason, probably because I got drunk, I wasn't where I was supposed to be, and I missed the bus. They found me still in the barrack, so I had to stay at the company for another six weeks waiting on orders. So finally, I got orders to Fort Sam Houston to be trained as a medic.

It worked out really well for me. We were all put in little groups to take tests to see what we were qualified for, and I scored high enough to be in leadership qualification. I was assigned a private room and got to march the guys to and from class. I also got a pass so I could leave base and go to town. I did classes for a medic and my MOS was a 2190B, which was an MOS for a combat medic. Then, of course, we all knew that our orders were going to be to Vietnam, so I was going to go in-country as a combat medic. The return rate was not very good for combat medics, and I realized that from my dad. He had been in combat during World War II and he had tears in his eyes when we got to the airport as I was leaving to go to Vietnam.

I didn't think anything good was going to come out of this, but I got lucky and got orders to the mail unit at Phu Bai, Vietnam. The 85th Mac is like a MASH unit like you have seen on TV. When I got up there, it was located a few miles south of Hue in I Corps. It was a hospital. It was going to be duty in a hospital instead of being in the bush, so I got lucky. The first thing I wanted to do was go to the club and have a beer. I went down and I was having a beer and one of the guys, John Kates, said, "You're one of the new guys, right?" I said I was, and he said they got all the medics they need in the hospital. "I can tell you right now you are either going to be assigned to be a gate guard or you're going to get my job as the mailman." He said it's the best job on the base. He said everyone likes you because you deliver the mail. "If you get the job, take care of those mess sergeants, they can do you a lot of favors. When you go in the office for review, they will ask you if you have any experience in delivering mail. Just raise your hand. Hell, they don't know. You can make up any story you want." It worked out just exactly like he said. I raised my hand, and I got a job in the mail room handing out the mail. It turned out it was the best job. Everyone smiled at you whether they liked you or not because you were the one carrying and delivering the mail and mail was the most important thing in Vietnam, getting letters from home.

At the base, the only time we got shot at was incoming missiles firing at the airport. Once in a while, we had to go out on the wire, but other

SP-4 Dwayne Williams, Phu Bai Base, 1970.

SP-4 Dwayne Williams, Phu Bai Base, 1970.

than that the duty was not real threatening. It wasn't like the guys coming into the hospital all shot up. There was a lot of them. Being around the ER you got to meet everybody, and you knew what the action was when the helicopters came in. It could have been anybody, including NVA, but it was mostly GIs—a lot of times in body bags. Sometimes we would have a big pile of them out there, a lot more than what the news was letting on. We were just one little evac hospital and damn we had a chopper landing all the time with wounded or full of body bags. I mean we were in the rear, so to speak. We had mama-sans taking care of our shoes and laundry. It was good duty compared to the guys coming in from the bush—they were dirty and filthy, and they didn't have anything as good as we had. I mean, we sure lost a bunch of guys, and it just didn't seem like the newspapers were keeping up with all the losses and what was really going on in the war.

When we were first there you weren't afraid of anything. When incoming would come in, if it was far enough away guys would get out and try to take photos of the explosions, but the shorter we got, the more we would head for the bunkers. No one wanted to take a chance on getting hit. Now, if the rockets were close, we would always head for the bunkers, but a lot of times they would be in the distance, so guys didn't worry about them then.

After we had been there for a while and before we got short, there was a lot of drugs. A lot of pot and cocaine, but it wasn't really cocaine—it was pure heroin. It was everywhere in little vials about the size of your little finger. You could buy it for three dollars.

I got in a little bit of trouble. I got busted twice for harboring Vietnamese nationals. I had a deuce-and-a-half, and I would go get girls and bring them on the compound and I could hide them in the truck. They would go to different hooches at the hospital and screw the GIs to make money. I never took any money myself from them. I got caught twice. I never got busted either time, but I never got promoted either. When I was up for E-5 they just didn't give me the stripe. I just got an ass-chewing for it. One time they called me in and said, "Williams, you're a married man. What would your wife think if she knew you were doing this?" I told them I don't know what she would think, but since she is halfway around the world, I don't think she is going to find out. I felt sorry for them. Their money wasn't any good anymore and they were really poor.

The sad part was all the body bags. A lot of those guys were burned up. We would call graves and they would come over. They had to open the bags to declare them dead and I saw a lot of doctors just puke their guts out. It was just terrible. We had a big lean-to like a shed where we put the bodies until graves got there, and sometimes they piled up pretty good.

It was I Corps area, and they were reporting we were shutting down with the activity. Shut down, my ass. There was a lot going on that just wasn't reported and stacks and stacks of bodies come through there.

We had a Bob Hope show once. John Bench was there one time. The Golddiggers. They had a lot of shows, and we had all the mama-sans taking care of us, had an NCO club, and stacks of bodies from the bush. It was like two different worlds. Other than a few rocket attacks, we were pretty safe, but we always had a lean-to of body bags. I only shot my rifle once when I was on the wire. We thought we saw something and opened up. I just took care of the truck and jeep, which included maintenance of changing tires and delivering all the mail.

I did go over when the choppers came in and helped unload the bodies. A lot of times it was more than I wanted to do. They had some new nurses that came in and they had a hard time at first with all the wounded and dead bodies. But they began to toughen up and became really good nurses. I saw one new nurse try to take the boot off a wounded soldier and

SP-4 Dwayne Williams and Gloria Loring from *The Bob Hope Show*, Phu Bai, 1970.

his foot came off his leg with the boot. She got really sick. We had to take her out of the dispensary till we could get her settled down. We had a lot that were wounded badly, and we did our best to help them. Arms or legs blown off and bad gunshot wounds, and we helped them the best we could. We saved a lot of them because we had a lot of good doctors and nurses.

When we started getting short, guys would want to throw parties for you. There were guys it was hard to say bye to, but we did, and we would say we will get together later. After I got home, I had a couple of guys call, but other than that I never did hook up with any of them. I just came home and melted back into society. No one wanted to talk about the war, and no one wanted to talk to me. That was a shocker. Locally no one wanted to buy you a beer or anything. It was like they just wanted to forget about it. They want to talk to you more now than they did then. I went to Williamsburg, Virginia, and I wore my Vietnam hat, and they just threw out the red carpet for me. They would do anything for you.

I tried school when I came home, but it didn't work out too well, so I went to work for the railroad. My brother was selling vacuum cleaners and I saw the kind of money he was making. He said come on out and try it. I did and I made $1,000 and I thought this was a lot better than what I was making at the railroad, so I quit the railroad to sell vacuum cleaners. My mom thought I had lost my mind. I did that till I turned 50, then I had a buddy that was involved in golf as a caddy. He wanted to know if I wanted to try it, so I went. The guy we were caddying for, J.C. Snead, was really good and ended up on the PGA tour. I ended up being a caddy for Sam Snead, J.C.'s uncle. I did that for 25 years until I retired.

Seven

SP-5 James E. Barnes, Dak To, 1967–68

1st Division, 8th Infantry Regiment, 8 HHC-D Co. and B Co., 4th Infantry Division

National Defense Medal, Vietnam Service Medal, Vietnam Campaign Medal, Combat Medical Badge, O/S, CMB, Rifle and Pistol Expert

August 15, 1967, I flew to South Vietnam with Bruce Andrews. It took us about all day—we left from Los Angeles, California, on this date. We flew into Cam Ranh Bay, then we flew to Pleiku. That took about 11 hours. We were treated very well because we were medics. We were both PFCs at that time. I took a Greyhound bus to California (two days—it was great but at the same time bittersweet). I met a lot of people and, considering the Vietnam War was unpopular, they were very good to us. But they were sorry we were going to 'Nam.

Bruce tells me we went to the mess hall and got some food—I think it was late. He remembers a soldier that was going home after his tour. He wished us luck and said that the 4th Infantry was a great unit to be with. The next morning, we went to the supply office and got our supplies, weapons, and medic materials—we had to sign for a morphine 10-pack that they placed in a cigarette box.

The next day we went and zeroed our M-16 Colt rifles and .45 Colt pistols. Our sergeant, Sergeant Kuck, was ready for us to come because D Company was coming into base that next day and Andrews and I were going to that company. D Company did come into Pleiku the next day. We all went out on patrol that night and set up a base camp near a river and a Mountain Yard (Montagnard) village. I pulled guard with a guy for one hour. It was the first night in the bush and I was nervous because I didn't know what to expect. Other than the mosquitoes, it was a quiet night with no contact.

The next morning, we got up and went to an airport and took a helicopter out to Duc Co.

We went into the Ia Drang Valley on one of our first missions. We went in with B Company, 1/8 Infantry. We patrolled the area and did not make any contact. I think we were there about two days and then we went back to a firebase and stayed for about four days and ran patrols out of the firebase.

Before I get too far with this, I would like to tell you a little bit about me. I went into the Army in September 1966. I went to Fort Polk in Louisiana for basic training for eight weeks. Then I went to Fort Sam Houston in Texas for 10 weeks of medical school along with Bruce and about eight other guys from Fort Polk.

After medic school (91B20) and individual combat medic training, we went to Fort Hood, Texas, and trained guys going to Vietnam. We did that for about July of 1967 and then we were given orders to go to Vietnam. Our sergeant told Andrews that we would go to work at a hospital. I knew that was not true because we were combat medics.

When we got to Vietnam, D Company was also just coming into the country. Guess where we went? D Company Infantry. New guys just coming in-country and straight to combat. We did not do much until September. We went to Duc Co and worked out of this area at first. September 13, 1967, I was wounded in the chest by one of our own guys, who said he saw NVA moving up on us. I was in his way, and he shot at them, but he shot me in the chest. I was out for about five minutes. It hit my dog tags and drove them into my chest at my heart.

The guy that shot me was also put on a helicopter and we went to the 71st Evacuation Hospital in Pleiku. He shot me with an M-79. I never talked to him again. I was put under a female doctor, and she took out my dog tags and patched me up. I was there about four days and I never had dog tags again. The morning after I was shot, three guys came into the hospital from D Company that had been wounded in an attack by NVA later on that afternoon. I knew two of them, Joe Edwards and Larry McAndress, but did not know the third guy.

Going back to Fort Hood, Andrews and I became closer. He went home with me, and I went home with him. We both lived in Texas. We did a lot of work together at Fort Hood. We trained soldiers going to Vietnam in war games. I wore street clothes, not Army clothes. We had a lieutenant that did not like me that much because I did things to him that made him look stupid. He was having problems with his appendix, and he wanted us to drive him to the hospital. He would not let me drive and he wanted to sit up front, so Andrews drove and I sat in the back seat. I had to stay with the jeep while Andrews took him in. That lieutenant was with HHC CO, and he gave us inspection about two weeks later. He knew who I was, and he passed me in the inspection. The lieutenant assigned Andrews and me to train new drivers for jeeps. That only lasted one day. After a happy hour, I think we tore up about five jeeps in one hour, but we did not stick around for all that; we just left. The lieutenant never said a word to us. I guess taking him to the hospital and all was worth it.

I never told Andrews, but I did not have to go to Vietnam because I was the only son in my family. I wanted to go because he was a great guy, and I could not let him go without me. My dad was the only son in his family, and he stayed in Washington, D.C., during World War II. I just could not stay at home and let my friend go. I wanted to be with him.

I met a lot of guys in Vietnam. Sergeant Kuck was the sergeant over the entire company. He liked me. After I got wounded, Dr. Tanner, our captain, wanted me to go back out in the bush the next next week. Sergeant Kuck wanted me to stay a few more days at base camp, but Captain Tanner got his way, so I went back out in the bush.

The first day we went out on a chopper, and it could not get close to the ground because of a tree. We had to jump about 15 feet to the ground. The jump hurt my chest a lot. I was so mad and hurt so bad I told my radio guy I wanted to go on patrol carrying a radio. The radioman was hurt also from the jump, and I gave him some aspirin and I took one too. I was madder than anything. I just wanted to shoot something. I was just mad because I was hurt. We went on patrol for the day and the only thing we saw were mosquitoes and the only thing I felt was pain in my chest and 120-degree temperature.

On the evening of September 13, D Company was two kilometers to the south of the fire support base. The signal was given to test-fire our weapons at our locations. A stray round from our mad minute [10 to 15 minutes of rapid fire) hit our senior medic (Williams) and he was picked up by our battalion commander. Seconds after he flew off, an estimated squad-size enemy force began firing small arms from the south. We were in contact for about 20 minutes. We had one killed and about four wounded. It was my first firefight.

About November 12, 1967, A Company was on a hill outside of Dak To. They were attacked by NVA on this hill, and I think they were there for two days. D Company was sent in the second morning to help, but by the time we got there, most of the fighting was over. They still had a fighter dropping rockets on the location where the NVA were located. We moved up on the location after the air strike and we ran into several NVA that had been wounded. I patched as many as I could and helped with all their needs. Then we were told that we needed to take the hill, so that is what we did. We only had several shots at us because when we got to the top of the

James Barnes (right) and Bruce Andrews at fire base Dak To.

hill, all that was there were dead NVA and body parts—arms, hands, legs, just dead NVA.

Our captain wanted us to move on looking for any NVA that hadn't been hit, so we headed north. We saw blood trails, but we did not see anything for about 300 yards on down the hill.

November 19, 1967, we were around Dak Klong, south of Hill 530. We engaged a good-sized NVA force for about an hour. We were ambushed and we had four guys killed and five wounded. It was the first time I heard "Medic!" in a firefight. I didn't have time to be scared. I just went for the wounded. I put pressure bandages on the bullet wounds and helped tag the dead and place them in body bags. We were north of Hill 1338 where 173rd Airborne and 3/12 4th Infantry were. At that time we were closer to Dak To. Joe Lyons was one of the guys killed; he was a great sergeant. He was wounded back on August 17, 1967, by our own artillery in a combat mission. He made it that time, but this time his luck ran out. The five guys that got hit received a Purple Heart. The families of the soldiers killed in action would receive the dead soldiers' Purple Hearts.

On December 4, 1967, D Company was coming into the firebase and NVA had placed a grenade on their path. It was set with a trip wire and hit by one of the guys coming into firebase. It went off, killing Sgt. William Hadley and Pfc. Albert Frazier and wounding about four other guys. One was Gordon Tubbs, and I was the only medic at this location. I did all the patching up for all of them and took care of the dead and took all of them to the choppers. Tubbs was the last guy I looked at because we thought he was dead. He came to about the time I was going to look at him. He was face down, so I did not know who it was until he tried to get up. The sergeant with me did not know it was Tubbs either. He had been about 20 yards from us before I got to him. He was coming around okay, but he had been hit pretty bad. I patched him up and walked him to the chopper. I did not see him until we made E-5 back at Pleiku about January. And then we went back out together with D Company. We went to Laos together and we saw a few more fights together. I think he was like me—he went to B Company and a few more before we went to Dak together about June of 1968. He went to Pleiku and was over medics coming into Vietnam. I stayed at Dak To and worked with Montagnard (Mountain Yards).

I also worked with recon for a short time. Lieutenant Newman wanted me to come to recon back when I got shot and I told him I would but David Hudson wanted to help with recon so I let him go with them. I did not think I would be going back as soon as I did.

One time Hudson was missing. He got cut off from the unit by NVA. He came back in about three days. We had looked for him, but he was hiding in the jungle from the NVA.

I try to stay in touch with Lieutenant Newman because I saw him all the time and I email about three of the guys that remember me from 'Nam.

One day we flew into a hill called Dog Bone. We were with C Company. We made contact with a supply unit for the

SP-5 James Barnes (left) and Gordon Tubbs at Firebase Dak To.

Sp-5 James Barnes with the village chief's son Sam at Dak To Base. He was brought in for treatment after being hit by an NVA grenade.

NVA. They were carrying guns, rice, and ammo. They fought us for about two hours and then they started running from us. They were carrying about two tons of rice and several weapons and ammo. We were told later they were one of the main units that carried ammo and food for the NVA.

One morning we were called to go help A Company, who was on a hill near Dak To. We got to the base of the hill in early morning and remained there while they conducted an air strike on the hill for about two hours. We got the word to move up the hill. As we moved up, we received light small arms fire. We returned fire and the NVA stopped shooting. We moved to the top of the hill and there was a lot of dead NVA soldiers. There were body parts everywhere—arms, legs, a couple of heads, and other parts. LT and I went up together along with our radio guy. We were the first squad up the hill, and about halfway up we saw an NVA soldier (we think he was an officer, because he had a sword). He waved the sword in the air. I had a clear shot at him but was told to hold up so I did. About two seconds later, he ran off and we never saw him again. I could have shot him in the leg. We went on up the hill, but we never saw anything or anyone else. We went on around to the road coming back into Dak To. We were out all day.

There were five soldiers from A Company that were wounded. I helped patch them up as best as I could to get them medevacked to an aid station. A good friend of mine, Landis Bargatze, thought I patched him up. I only know Landis because of the incident on the hill [with the VC who had the sword]. I attended a conference with the 4th Division a few years ago and was with Wendell Conners, another medic from Company A, and he said he was the one that patched Landis up.

I think the first time I saw Conners was when A and D Companies met one day, and we stayed together for a couple of days. Conners was a medic that arrived in the unit the same time as I did. He and three other guys came into camp with a 12-foot snake they had caught. They cooked it that night and gave us some of it. It was very good. The guy who cooked it was from Hawaii and had cooked snake several times before coming to Vietnam.

The next time I saw Conners was about June of '68, about two months before we went home. We worked together helping Montagnard northwest of Dak To. Conners was the best medic I ever worked with because he took care of everyone. He worked very hard in the villages helping the kids and all the villagers. He had a big heart.

The last time I saw Conners was July 2012, when he came down to Texas and, along with Kenny [also in my unit], who lives in San Antonio, Texas, visited my house. We went to Greenville, Texas, and went to my old high school and then to Dallas to visit the Kennedy Museum.

My second time in the Ia Drang Valley, it was a very dark night. There was no moon and I think it was the darkest night I spent in Vietnam. You could hold your hand out and couldn't see it. Our point men saw several NVA soldiers walk right up to each other. Our guys killed three of them and we pulled back to camp. We thought we were going to be attacked so we made ready for it, but the attack never came. We heard movement all night but did not see anything to shoot at. All of us stayed on guard all night and the next morning we moved about 1,000 yards forward from our position and set up again, but we did not make any contact that night either.

I remember us going over into Laos because we heard the NVA was setting up there. We also wanted to check out the Ho Chi Minh Trail for movement. We spent two days over there and we heard a lot of movement. We heard tanks and trucks moving south. We could also hear trees falling.

Seven. James E. Barnes

Sp-5 James Barnes at Mountain Yard near Dak To.

We did not make contact with them because we were not supposed to be in Laos.

Coming out of Laos, we ran into a bunker of the NVA. We had one guy that was five foot five and he went down into the bunker but could not see anything, so we blew it up with C-4. The guy was not a tunnel rat, but we called him one after he went into the tunnel. The next morning after returning from Laos, we called in a B-52 strike on the locations where we heard movement.

We had a battle one day and had four soldiers killed. The NVA was everywhere. I was pulled out of field to the aid station. We had so many soldiers that had been brought into the aid station that I was put in charge of seeing as many of them as I could and to assist the five doctors who were at the station. It was not a great job, but they wanted me to do it. I would say that 90 percent of these soldiers were from 173 Airborne. I had a few guys that died on me. I had a priest that never left my side. He was a lot of help. One soldier who was shot in the head asked me to tell his mother what had happened and then he died. I went to the next soldier. I would say that we had about 30 that came to the aid station that day. Several died as I worked on them. All the training in the world cannot prepare you for the mental strain it puts on you.

During my last two months in 'Nam, I wanted to go to a Montagnard (Mountain Yard) village just about a mile north of Dak To. I had made plans about a week before Conners and Richardson had come into Dak To. I had made plans with about six other guys that were going home in about 10 days. They said they would go and cover us. We had about 15 guys that went out with us. The day we went out, this village got hit by the NVA. We got there just as the NVA moved out, but we did not hear any shots, so we did not know what had gone on as we went into the village. We were surprised by what had happened. We had about four that had been killed and several that had been wounded. The chief of the village had been killed and his son had been wounded by a grenade. He had some shrapnel in him, and I took out as much as I could and patched him up. I had one villager that died later on, but we patched up most of them, maybe eight or more. We went back out to the village about two days later to check on the wounded. Conners was very good at taking care of all the sick, so I let him take care of them. I tried to make friends with all the kids. I noticed that the chief's son was not doing too good, so I took him in with me to base camp in Dak To. Doc Tanner took a look at him and X-rayed his face because he thought that he had some frags in his chin. The X-ray showed there was a small piece in his lower chin, and we took it out. He was out for about two hours. I took him back to my tent. I kept him with me until I had to go home. When it was time for me to leave, no one would keep him and I had to take him back to the village. It was the hardest thing I had to do in the war!

A few years after I got home, I started to try to find soldiers I was with in 'Nam. I found some, mostly guys from Company D, but a few from A, B, and C Companies too. The 4th Infantry Division meets every year and I have gone for the last three years. I meet with some guys that were in recon. Lieutenant Newman was my buddy in 'Nam, and I email him almost every day. He is a great guy. Bruce Andrews was my best friend in the Army. Tubbs was also a good friend. Wendell Conners was the best and Richardson is still a great guy. I have about 100 guys' email addresses and I hear from almost all of them. I try to see them a couple of times a year.

Something I should say about the Vietnam War: none of us had names on our uniforms. We did not know others' names that well. Medics knew medics, but we did not know names like the infantrymen. They had been together for a while and we medics were just added to the unit. We had to read dog tags for names of guys shot or killed. I only did that once. After that I told them that the guys at base camp could get names. I just tried to patch them up.

Time has been good to me. I served in 'Nam. I was hit in the chest by an M-79, had malaria twice, spent my 21st birthday in 'Nam, and survived many firefights. I was lucky. I came home, but many didn't. I keep in touch with as many of the guys that I can now. They know the true meaning of "I got your back."

Eight

SP-5 John M. Maag, Dak To, Pleiku, 1967–68

1st Division, 8th Infantry Regiment, 4th Infantry Division
Army Commendation Medal with Valor, Combat Medical Badge, South Vietnam Cross of Gallantry with Bronze Star

I was drafted in 1966 and I went in the Army officially in June 1966. I took my basic training at Fort Ord in California, and while I was there, they offered us three choices. I could be either a cook, MP, or medic. I didn't know how to cook. My father had been a big gambler and he wasn't too fond of the police, so I decided to become a medic. After basic training they sent me to Fort Riley, Kansas, to Irwin Army Community Hospital, which is where I trained. That was very unusual because almost all the medics went to Fort Sam Houston for medic training. I trained there from October 1966 through May 1967. In addition to my medic training, I cross-trained as a pharmacist and worked at a dispensary for about three months. At that time, I was in the 1st Infantry Division in the 3rd Armored Unit. We had these experimental tanks that were very unusual. They shot a high-explosive round that had a fiberglass casing and everything blew out the barrel. There was no casing coming back and the tank could also shoot a guided missile. We were training to go over as a unit. I think there were 1,000 men in the unit. They were still testing the tank down at Fort Hood, Texas, and they started getting cook off rounds and the explosions actually killed some of the tankers, so they scrapped the project and scrapped the idea of going to Vietnam as a unit. Instead, everyone was individually sent to be assigned to different units. Some went to the 1st Division, some went to the 4th Division, and some to the 9th Division. I was assigned to the 4th Division.

In June 1967 I flew into Cam Ranh Bay and then they flew us into Pleiku, which was in the Central Highlands. I was there about 10 days.

It was raining heavily with monsoons every day. Then they moved me, two other medics, and some infantrymen out to B Company, 1st Division of the 8th Infantry. They had just been in one of the biggest battles in Vietnam, which took place in May 1967. The story was they had five medics when the battle started and when it was over, they only had one medic left.

Two other medics and I flew out to B Company. It was still raining constantly and did so up till November 1967. Basically, we went on search-and-destroy missions every day. The routine was we would wake up before sunlight, maybe five in the morning. We were carrying all our gear rucksacks. I had a special forces pack in which I carried several aid kits, and it weighed about 80 pounds. The infantrymen were carrying rucksacks that weighed over 100 pounds. We would start early in the morning and walk all day. The only break we would take might be for 15 minutes while the captain was getting his map coordinates. Then we would get to our destination, dig a foxhole, cut trees for overhead protection, and carry sandbags that we filled with the dirt and make two layers around the foxholes in case we received a mortar attack. At night we would put out our listening points. Everyone had to pull LP for at least an hour each night with the radio. The medics were the only ones that didn't have to pull duty on the LP, so I never had to do it. Every morning we would start over and do the same thing. At one time we did this every day over 60 days and it was all in mountains. It was pretty tough.

We had a high rate of malaria. Everyone was taking their pills, but the troops were so worn from the constant walking that their body resistance was much lower, and the pills were not working. One time they sent

SP-5 John Maag, Mountains of Dak To, 1967.

out this major from one of the hospitals to see why our malaria rate was so high. The major wasn't used to going through a routine and he was only with us one day. He had a rucksack with about 40 pounds of equipment with him and before we reached our destination for that night, we had to take his rucksack and divide up his equipment and carry it for him. Then when we got to our destination for the night, he had the captain call in a helicopter and get him out of there not even after one day. When he was getting on the chopper, I was the head medic then and I told him that when he got back to tell them this is why so many are getting malaria. They are so run down that the pills don't work. The troops' body resistance was too low to fight it off.

God was looking after us because we would go into an area and nothing would happen and then we would leave and another unit would come in and they would get into a massive firefight or we would go in areas where there had been big battles and the NVA would be gone. Starting in November there were some big battles. The 38th Infantry had a couple of companies that were overrun. One of my high school classmates got killed in Dak

SP-5 John Maag (left) and Richard Penney, Mountains of Dak To, 1967.

To. He was in the infantry. What was happening was the NVA was starting to move down south because they were preparing for the Tet Offensive. It was one of the best-kept military secrets and we couldn't figure out why we couldn't find the NVA. We were going after the NVA 33rd Regiment and we kept walking around unable to locate them.

There was one incident in December 1967 where we saw these lights going through this canyon and we tried to call in artillery on them, but the command post said they would not do a fire mission unless we made contact with them to make sure they were NVA because they were over budget on ammunition. The day after we saw these lights and they had denied us a fire mission an infantry company made contact with the NVA unit, and one platoon got cut off. Some got away but the lieutenant stayed with the wounded till help came. We were going to go rescue them. We had a platoon and me and we were going to go up this hill and rescue them but they called off the mission because they said the NVA had overrun the position and had killed everybody. I always felt that had they let us have the fire mission, the NVA wouldn't have been in condition to overrun any of our units and those men would not have been killed.

A lot of crazy things happened in 'Nam. One time we flew into this Christmas Tree Hill and there was an artillery unit there. The hill had been occupied before and there was a trench that had been dug around the top of it. The NVA hit the hill with artillery rounds and the men on the hill abandoned their posts and ran down into the trench, but there was a guy that was trapped at the top and was wounded. There were ammo boxes stacked up and they were on fire. The medic for their unit was in the trench and he threw his medical bag out of the trench and refused to go help the wounded soldier. He threw the medical bag out so basically anyone who wanted to grab it and go help the wounded guy could, but he wasn't doing it. They called us for help. One of the infantrymen and myself went up the hill. Fortunately for us as when we were going up the hill, they stopped shooting rockets. When we got up to the top of the hill, we saw the artilleryman had a wound in his leg, but it wasn't too bad. We saw the ammo boxes on fire. We grabbed the guy and dragged him back down the hill. I just thought it was crazy how this medic had just abandoned his men. They gave me and the infantryman medals for rescuing the artilleryman. The infantryman got a Bronze Star and because I was a medic, and it was my job, I got the Army Commendation Medal with a V for valor. The crazy thing was I got a Silver Star from the South Vietnamese government for it. I talked to a lot of guys and none of them knew of anyone getting a Silver Star from the South Vietnamese government.

When we were in Dak To guarding the airbase, the NVA were shooting in these 122 mm rockets almost every night just before the sun went down. The first one came in when we were guarding the perimeter and hit the airstrip, which was covered with medal, and blew a huge hole in it. There was a general there and he called up the powers that be and said, "Hey, the Air Force dropped a bomb on our airstrip. What's going on here?" They told him they hadn't dropped any bombs. It continued every night. Those rockets would go through five layers of sandbags, which is what we had to cover our positions.

Then from another hill they started shooting 75 recoilless rockets every night. The general had 15 to 20 layers of sandbags over his command. He told us to go up on the mountain they were shooting the rockets from and see if we could find them. The next day we were going up into the mountains in two flanks and all of a sudden three NVA came out of a bunker actually between our flanks. They ran through one of our lines and our captain, who was kind of a crazy guy, started chasing them for some odd reason, and one of our machine gunners opened fire trying to hit the NVA, but he almost killed the captain. The guy's name was Felix because he looked like the car salesman in California who owned Felix Chevrolet. The captain came back and he was all pissed off. He yelled at Felix, "What the hell were you doing? Didn't you see me there?" It was pretty much the captain's fault because he darted out chasing the NVA. That's like a crazy thing to do.

In Dak To, we always set up on a mountain. The idea was to dig foxholes. If the NVA came after us, they had to go uphill. We were set up on this hill and we got word they were going to do a B-52 strike. It was about five in the morning and it wasn't light yet, and all of a sudden I heard this whining sound and thought the NVA were shooting rockets at us. I bolted out of the tent and the mosquito net was covering me and I just ran and jumped in the foxhole. The sound was a 1,000-pound bomb from a B-52 that had hung up and then dropped near our position. It killed one of the LPs—we were lucky that was all—but it lit up the whole sky. If that bomb had landed in the middle of our perimeter, it would have killed 20 or 30 of us at least. After the B-52 strike, we went down into the valley, and we didn't find one NVA body. I talked to a lot of other guys and that had been pretty much the case when they dealt with the bombings. Either the NVA knew about them, or we had bad intelligence because the B-52 bombings just weren't very effective.

One time in the field we had friendly artillery fire that mistakenly landed on top of us. I had a friend that went to the same high school I did and was one year older. We were going up this hill and a 105 mm round landed right between his legs but it was a dud and it did not go off. It would have killed him and who knows how many of the other infantry. Another time we were up by Dak To and they told us to build this massive medical bunker because they said we were going to get hit and we needed to have a bunker for the wounded. We started blowing up these trees with dynamite and then we dug this massive hole, maybe 25 feet square, and then dug down maybe eight feet. We took the trees we had blown and laid them over the hole, then covered those with about five layers of sandbags. It took us several days to build it. No sooner had we finished it than we got word to disassemble it—we were moving out.

Another time we were blowing an LZ so the choppers could bring us in supplies. There was one huge tree that was about 50 or 60 feet high, so the guys put this dynamite around the tree. A chopper had dropped some C rations in, and guys were picking them up and the guys on the tree just yelled "Fire in the hole" and blew the tree up. A bunch of guys got splinters in them, and the tree actually fell on one infantryman and he was hurt really bad. He went into shock. I went over to him, and he was whitish-gray. I actually talked him out of shock. I told him he was going to be okay. We called a medevac, and I told them he wanted to get up but when you get him to the aid station, get him in right away and don't let him walk or move around until he is checked out. I found out the next day that he talked to the guys on the medevac and convinced them he was okay and instead of doing what I told them to do they let him walk into the aid station and he sat down. They were going to check him out and there were other wounded soldiers that needed care and he told them he was okay, take care of the others first. Once they got back to him, he was dead. He had a ruptured spleen.

SP-5 John Maag putting foot powder on Vietnamese girl, road to Dak To, 1967.

There were other friendly fire incidents that happened. I think most of us were equally afraid of the NVA and friendly fire. One time we went out on patrol with about 15 infantrymen and we were on this ridgeline above a valley, and we heard these voices down in the valley. I was a specialist 5 by then and there was a buck sergeant, and we were the highest ranking on the patrol. He said he was going to call in mortars because the artillery would have just gone over the valley. He gave the coordinates over the radio and the first mortar round went too far. The second mortar round landed in back of us. I was looking at him and he was looking at me and said don't do it. We agreed to cancel the mission because we were afraid the third round would land on top of us.

One time we were on patrol, and we had gone off this mountain and into some flat land. We were going through the jungle and all of a sudden, the area all opened up. We thought what the heck is this and it looked like a big trail. It was about 35 yards wide. We learned we were on the Ho Chi Min Trail. We started walking on the trail and actually ended up in Cambodia. Our captain called up and gave our coordinates so we could be resupplied. He was informed we were in Cambodia, and we were not getting resupplied until we moved back into South Vietnam. They told us we had 1,000 NVA moving toward us. We needed to get back into Vietnam and set up a perimeter. They were going to send out another company for support. We moved back into Vietnam and set up the perimeter. We dug foxholes and made covers over them. We were sure we were going to be hit. They started sending extra troops for reinforcement. We had this one staff sergeant that flew in; his name was Willie Holden. He was a Black staff sergeant and after he got in there we were sitting around on some logs and eating C rations, and someone said, "There's the 1-6, he is the head medic." He came up to me and said, "I'm Willie Holden and I'm a staff sergeant and I'm going to be your platoon sergeant," and I said, "Yeah, I'm the head medic." He asked me, "Well, where did you take your training?" I said, "Training? I'm a cook. They killed all the other medics, so they just gave me an A-bag and told me to go out to the infantry." And I said, "Sarge, if anything happens, maybe you could give me a few pointers." He went crazy. He stood up and he started yelling, "I want out of here now." He went up to the captain and the captain asked what was going on, and the sarge said, "Your head medic isn't even a medic—he is a cook." The captain called me over and said, "Okay, Maag, what have you been telling Sergeant Holden?" and I said, "Well, Captain, I was just having some fun," and he said, "Knock that shit off." We just tried to have some fun out there because the situation was pretty bad most of the time.

Everyone had nicknames. There was this one guy who was only 18 years old and we called him Nancy Sinatra because he had a picture of

Nancy Sinatra. She sang the song "These Boots Are Made for Walkin'." One day we were out in the jungle, and we were taking a break and there were these two guys from Flint, Michigan, and they were machine gunners. Louis and Nagley were their names, and they were really white trash. Every other word out of their mouths was a cuss word. I asked them what they thought about Vietnam. And they said they really aren't doing anything any different than they did back home except for shooting at people and getting paid for it. The story was for them it was either go into the military or they were going to jail. But back to Nancy Sinatra... About five of us were sitting on this log, including Nancy Sinatra. Louis and Nagley were just trashing her, she was nothing but a whore and on and on, and Nancy Sinatra just started crying and he grabbed his M-16 and was going to shoot them. We had to fight him to get his M-16 away from him. I told these guys not to do that again, he would probably kill them if no one was there to stop him. He was a very immature guy that went AWOL when he went on R&R. It took like 10 days to find him.

The captain when we were on patrol in the jungle always wanted me up with him. I didn't think it was a good idea because he had two radiomen with him and the artillery officer and I thought I should be back from them, so when we would get to moving I would work my way back away from them. I always liked to walk with the Black soldiers because they didn't seem to be as uptight as everyone else. They were always joking around. There was one Black guy from New Jersey, and he was always trashing everybody, including me. We had a lot of fun together. There were never any racial issues at all. I saw only one fight the entire time I was in the field, and it was between two white guys.

We were up at Dak To in an unusual area. It was triple canopy with vines, trees, and bamboo. Some of the trees were 60 feet high and the bamboo was big, maybe 40 feet high, and really thick. The vines were on the top. On one occasion we were in a hill area but there was a lot of grass, like really high, maybe three feet high, and we sent out this patrol and all of a sudden, we heard this gunfire and our captain, who was a gung-ho guy, got on the radio and asked what was happening out there. There was this kid Paco Bryson out there and he was from the San Fernando Valley, California. He was the leader of the squad that went out on patrol and the kid said, "We got one." And the captain said, "You got one?" He confirmed they did. The captain told him to bring him in. Paco said okay and the captain was so excited he called "the Bullet," who was our command; he was a lieutenant colonel. He told him we got an NVA and the lieutenant colonel said he was going to come in. The lieutenant colonel gets on his helicopter and comes in and lands. The captain is talking to him and we were all waiting in a defensive position, not knowing what was going to happen. We thought we were going to get hit. The captain calls on the radio and asked what was taking them so long and the squad leader told him that they were getting a bamboo pole to carry him in. It was a long time and then in came the squad leader out of the grass and into the perimeter and the guys have this bamboo pole with some rope attached to it and there was about a six-foot lizard attached to this pole. Oh, when the captain saw this he just went berserk, screaming, "What the hell, you 'got one'?" The squad leader said, "Yes, we did, and here it is." The lieutenant colonel looked at the captain like he was some kind of nut. He just gave the captain a dirty look and got on his helicopter and left. Then the captain for about five minutes just screamed at the squad leader telling him what kind of idiot he was. It was one of the funniest things I saw when I was there.

A couple of times I had the first sergeant try to take over being the head medic. The infantrymen were cutting overhead cover and one of them slashed himself with a machete and he had really cut his lower leg pretty bad, and I took a look at it. It definitely needed stitches and I didn't have anything to do stitches with so I was going to send him in because out there if you had any kind of open cut it would just get infected right away. I said we need to get this guy out of here and get him back to the base camp to get stitched up. The first sergeant said, "Wait a minute, let me take a look at that." They made me take the bandage off so he could look at it and then he said, "Oh, he doesn't need to go. We don't need to call a helicopter in for that." I told him, "Oh really, where did you take your medical training?" He said, "Well, I didn't take medical training," and I said, "That's right, you didn't. I decide who's going in, not you." He got really mad and said he was going to get me court-martialed for disobeying an order. He went up to the captain and started giving the story and I told the captain that I said he needed to go in. The captain told the first sergeant that they had to go by what the medic said, not him. Boy, the first sergeant was pissed.

Another time we had been working by this village and some of the guys had been with some of the Vietnamese women and two of the guys came down with the clap. They were both in the same squad and their lieutenant was useless and lazy. He never even dug his own foxhole. His men would dig his foxhole every night. Anyway, when I saw these two guys in his squad had the clap, I knew we needed to send them in. They needed shots and the lieutenant said no, let them suffer, let them stay out here. I said okay. When I sent someone in I had to fill out this EMT card with their name and the diagnosis so the medics in the rear would know what condition to treat. I filled two cards out for them, and I told the lieutenant I was going to send them in, and he said, "No, I told you they are not going to go in." I said, "Okay, here is what I am going to do. I want you to sign these cards that if these men become sterile because you left them out here, you're going to be personally responsible." He said he knew I was not going to do that. I said, "Okay, if you're not going to sign it, they are going in." I sent them in anyway. He was from South Carolina and a real clown. We had some good officers, and we had some that were just useless. We were fortunate that we had about five NCOs that had had combat experience in Korea and those were the guys that the men looked up to.

Another interesting story: we were in Dak To guarding the perimeter. It was another occasion when some of the guys had got a hold of some of these Vietnamese women. There were these three Black soldiers and in the morning, they brought this Vietnamese woman up to me and said, "Hey, Doc, what's wrong with this gal?" I looked at her and determined she had smallpox. I asked them if they had been sleeping with her and they said yes, she had been with them all night. I said, "Wow, she has smallpox." They asked what that meant. I said, "You guys are going to be dead within 24 hours." They go, "What?" I said, "What do you expect? Smallpox is deadly." Their faces just dropped. I said, "You better go back and write your parents because this is going to be your last letter. Put down everything you need to say." I let them go back and I waited for about 10 minutes and then I went and told them it wasn't fatal but don't do it again.

Another time in Dak To, the NVA were shooting in these 20 mm rockets, and they would blow a hole about 20 meters in diameter. I was in the medic headquarters and this captain came in and said, "I want you to write me up for a Purple Heart," and I asked what happened. Around a lot of the tents they had these wooden ammo boxes stacked and filled with sand to make a wall around the tent. The captain had gotten a splinter in his ass from one of the ammo boxes when a rocket came in. He said he would show me. I said, "No need, I'm not going to write you up for a Purple Heart." He said, "Why? I got wounded." I said, "I don't give a shit about you getting a splinter in your ass. There's guys out there getting shot." I said, "No, you're going to have to find someone else."

When I was out in the field, I made some enemies. The first sergeant hated me and the first lieutenant hated me. We had a doctor in charge of headquarters, and he came out to the field and we were at the firebase. He was going to bring all the guys' shot cards up to date. He came out with some medics from the headquarters and had all the guys' records. He said they were going to give all the guys shots. I told him I thought we should give our guys the shots. He got really upset about that. He let us do it, but he let me know he wasn't happy about it. He went back and after six months the medics were supposed to rotate out of the field so at the end of December, they didn't replace me. Then at the end of January, they didn't replace me again. I think he was going to just leave me out there to get killed because I had pissed him off. God was looking out for me because in February 1968 they sent me into Dak To the main base camp. They had sent me in for supplies and the doctor who hated me had been replaced. The new doctor was Captain Tanner from California and he introduced himself to me. He asked if by chance I played chess. I told him when I was young, I used to play a lot of chess with my brother and friends but I hadn't played in a couple of years. He said, "Well, why don't you play me. I have played everyone else and have beat them." I said, "Well, it's probably not going to be a match," and he said, "Well, just play me anyway." We played and I actually beat him. I think I caught him off guard; it was a pretty short game. I went back out to the field, and I got to thinking about how that wasn't a very smart thing to do. The other captain was mad at me and now I just beat the new captain in chess. I was never going to get out of the field. However, a couple of weeks later he transferred me out of the field, but he never played chess with me again.

They transferred me back from Dak To to Pleiku and I ran a Civil Affairs team for about four months. I was in charge of about four infantrymen, and we went out to three Mountain Yard villages. What we would do is get a jeep and a deuce-and-a-half and drive out to these three villages and pull MEDCAPs every day. It was pretty interesting visiting the Montagnard (Mountain Yards). I really liked them. The story with the Mountain Yards was they were run out of the south part of Vietnam by the South Vietnamese, and they went up to the northern part of Vietnam in the Central Highlands by Pleiku. They looked like miniature Indians. They wore only loin cloths. The women wore like a shirt, but they were topless. They were hunters. They went out and hunted small game, they grew pineapples, they grew rice. They were very friendly and loved the GIs, but they hated the South Vietnamese because the South Vietnamese ran them out of the most fertile part of the land. They lived out in the plains, not in the jungles. When we went out for the MEDCAPs, they always had something going on, like a funeral or wedding, and they used to drink this rice wine out of a vase with bamboo straws. The higher-ups told us not to drink the rice wine. There had been four or five Civil Affairs teams that had been going out every day to some of the villages and some of the guys had drunk the wine and came down with hepatitis. The problem was if you didn't drink it with them, they considered it a total insult.

One time we were celebrating with them inside a hutch, and they had a fire going and they brought in this dead dog. The dog had the fur on it, and they threw this dog on the fire. It started smoldering and the hair was burning off of it, and there is nothing that smells worse than burning hair. It was a horrible smell. After it burned off, they started cutting up this dog. I was eating part of this dog leg. It was really difficult to celebrate with him.

One day I was out at this village and this old man came up and was pointing to his mouth. I looked in there and saw a rotted tooth. I had an interpreter with me, and I said, "What's he want me to do?" The interpreter said, "He wants you to pull his tooth out." I said, "I don't have any novocaine," and he said, "No, he wants you to pull it. Don't worry about the pain." I had this pair of forceps, and I just went in there and grabbed hold of the tooth and I pulled it out and then I gave him some peroxide and told him to swirl it around in his mouth and spit it out. The interpretation did not go well, and he swallowed it. He started to puke. The next day I went back there and there were like 15 men lined up wanting me to pull their teeth out. I did the best I could. Some of them I could pull out and some of them broke off. Some of the teeth were rotten and I just couldn't get everything out. These guys were tough as nails. They never made a sound. No pain meds or anything and they just stood there and took it.

Another time when we went out, we had an interpreter with us but this one village had a chief and he was a very smart guy. He could speak five languages—English, French, Vietnamese, and two of the dialects of the Mountain Yards. We went out to this one village, and he said this one lady was dying. He wanted me to look at her. She was about 30 years old and not moving at all. She was barely breathing, and I gave her shots of penicillin. Two days later we came back, and I thought she was going to be dead by then. I asked the chief how the lady was, and he said she was gone and I said I was sorry she died and he said no and pointed out in this field, and there she was walking around with this big basket on her shoulders. I thought about it and these people had never had any antibiotics in their lives and it really had a great effect on them.

Another one day when I went out there was a kid that was really sick. He was maybe eight months old. He had a bad cut on his foot. I put some meds on it, and I stitched it up the best I could. Before I stitched him up, this Mountain Yard gave me this egg. It was a duck's egg. They wanted me to eat it. I didn't want to eat it, so I told them I'd eat it later and I put it in my front pocket. I was putting the meds on this kid's foot and he kicked me and it broke the egg. It was the most horrible smell. I thought I was going to puke.

I really liked working with them. They really liked Americans and appreciated anything we did for them. One of the chiefs wanted me to marry his daughter, which is considered a real honor with their customs. I brought back a bunch of artifacts. I had a crossbow, a machete (at one time they were headhunters), some baskets, and blankets they handmade. I actually still have some of it.

After about four months of dealing with the villagers, I was about to leave Vietnam. I was at Cam Ranh Bay doing paperwork and I got very sick. I was good at diagnosing the different kinds of malaria and there was another disease called dengue fever. I felt really bad, but I didn't want to let on that I was sick because I didn't want to get stuck in Vietnam. They flew us to Fort Lewis in Washington and after a day or so I started feeling better. Thank God I found out I had dengue fever and not malaria.

At Fort Lewis we started processing out and we were going from building to building filling out different paperwork and getting our final pay. We were walking one morning, and we had some guys that had been wounded and were in bad shape and weren't getting along very well. We had this lieutenant that was marching us, and he was calling out cadence and I told him he had guys here that could barely walk. The lieutenant got very upset at me. When I went to get my final papers, I went to the window, and they said my papers had been lost. They were trying to screw me for what I had said to the lieutenant. I had to stay in this room for about six hours and finally they said they had found my paperwork. The tradition in the Army is your last meal is supposed to be a steak dinner. They actually had a couple of mess halls set up and I went over and had steak, baked potato, and green beans. My last meal in the Army.

I got on a bus to the airport, and I flew from Fort Lewis, Washington, to LA International Airport. Then I took a Greyhound bus from there to Glendale, and when I got off the bus, I was about a mile away from my house. I walked the rest of the way home. I got to my parents' house, and I knocked on the door. My mom opened the door, and she was so happy to see me. She said, "Why didn't you tell us you were coming?" I didn't have a good answer, but I was there.

I was 21 years old then and for four or five years I did odd jobs. I worked for the city of Glendale, worked with a concrete crew. I met my wife, Eileen, when I was 25. We got married in June 1973 and then I went to school on the G.I. Bill for about four years. I was a chemistry major, and I wanted to work at this job as a chemical salesman, and while waiting this company offered me a job in insurance. I didn't know anything about insurance, but a friend said just go into it for three months and if you don't like it you can go for the other job. In the meantime, my wife got pregnant and if I took the chemical job I would have had to travel and I didn't want to do that so I stayed with the insurance company for five years. Then in 1979, I left the company to form my own insurance business called John M. Maag Insurance Services. I still run it today.

We had two children. My son, Jeffery, unfortunately, died on June 9, 1996, when he was 18, which was a heartbreaker. I have a daughter, Kristen. She is married and I have three grandchildren: Angela, age 10; Paco, age 6; and Christian, age 4. I think God for all my blessings and for sparing my life in Vietnam because I never thought I was going to get out alive.

The most disappointing thing is the way the war ended. The Paris Peace Treaty was nothing but a slam. The U.S. basically forced the South Vietnamese to sign the treaty, which allowed the North Vietnamese not to remove their troops from the south. To me it was the writing on the wall. What peace treaty would allow the enemy to remain in your country? After the treaty, the North Vietnamese came down the road of Saigon and took over the capital and then the country. Our air support could have wiped out the NVA, but we did nothing. Then they tortured a lot of the South Vietnamese soldiers. Why didn't they do like they did in Korea? It was just sad. We lost over 50,000 men and just let them walk in and take the country.

NINE

Staff Sergeant Alfred Penn Davidson, Pleiku, January 1969–December 1969

1ST BATTALION, 8TH INFANTRY REGIMENT, COMPANY B, 4TH INFANTRY DIVISION

Vietnam Service Medal, Vietnam Campaign Medal, National Defense Medal, 2 Silver Stars with Combat V, Air Medal, Army Commendation Medal, Good Conduct Medal, Rifle and Pistol Expert

I grew up in Delaware in a very poor environment. I was raised by my mother near my uncle's farm when I was little. My mother was killed in a car accident and after that I was bounced around from family to family. I graduated high school and I got a job in a restaurant as a manager and worked at that for about a year. I was getting close to being drafted so I decided to enlist in the Army. I enlisted in the Army in 1967 and I went to Fort Bragg, North Carolina, for basic training. After that I went to Fort Sam Houston for what I call combat medic training, but also nurses training with an MOS of 91C, which would be a nurse. I knew when I went in the Army I wanted to save lives and I wanted to serve my country.

During the year of 1968, I was stationed at Fort Myer, which is near Arlington National Cemetery across the Potomac River from Washington, D.C. I worked at an outpatient clinic that predominantly took care of the families of the military service personnel. During that time, Martin Luther King was killed and there were riots in Washington, D.C. I was assigned a jeep and driver military support with numerous military men and we were based at police precinct number. We went out and saw people breaking into and burning stores. We were shot at numerous times and the jeep driver would turn around and head away from the shots being fired the best he could. On one of the trips, we went back to the police station and noticed there were piles and piles of shoes, clothing, and everything else the rioters had taken. The police had taken it away from them. We could take what we wanted out of the stacks and I got a new pair of shoes and a new jacket out of it.

We went back down to Washington, D.C., in the jeep and this time we took a box of tear gas grenades with us. And as we patrolled the streets, if we saw the rioters looting we would take the tear gas grenades and throw them inside the shop or store or whatever they were in. Eventually the riots were under control, but not before a lot of the city had been burned and a lot of looting and destruction had occurred.

During that same year, Robert F. Kennedy was shot and killed. His funeral was being held in New York and then his body was being transported to Washington, D.C., by train to be buried at Arlington National Cemetery. I was assigned to a presidential ambulance to be parked at the cemetery for support of the presidential family in the event that anything happened during the funeral. We got to the cemetery late morning, about 11:00 a.m. The train left New York and took hours and hours to get to Washington, D.C., because of all the people who were getting on the train tracks. It ended up he was buried about 10:30 that night with lights that had been placed at the cemetery because it was dark. However, we did not have to render any assistance to anyone during the burial.

Also during the time I was there, they had a big demonstration at the Pentagon. There were thousands of people and I called them hippies. We had an ambulance over there. It was a Cadillac ambulance, and the hippies came over and were trying to steal the ambulance. I, along with a couple other guys, got the hell beat out of us fighting these guys, but they didn't get the ambulance. However, they did steal the stretcher out of the back. The next day the colonel wanted to know how we let the hippies get the stretcher from the ambulance.

I was at Fort Myer for about a year and then I got orders to go to Vietnam two days before Christmas and I shipped out to go in-country in January 1969. I had orders to be a nurse in a hospital in Long Behn. I arrived at Cam Ranh Bay to check in for my assignment. They gave me a rifle and all the combat equipment and told me to get on this helicopter. It didn't make any sense to me, but I did as I was told. Then I was informed that I was assigned to the 1st Battalion, 8th Infantry, B Company, 4th Infantry Division. We took off in the helicopter and flew to a firebase in the middle of nowhere. I got off the helicopter along with two other guys. I had no idea what was going on, but I was pretty pissed off that I had been assigned to the infantry company since I had orders to report to the hospital in Long Behn.

After I got to the firebase, I was assigned to some living quarters. That night the entire firebase was overrun by the NVA. There were firefights and

SSG Penn Davidson at the aid station, Dak To, 1969.

explosions all around me. I helped many soldiers that were hit that night, patching them up going from one after the other. We finally ran the NVA off and the fighting stopped. We had a lot of soldiers killed that night and I had to ID them and put them in body bags. I found it strange that they had a number of body bags available at the firebase. I spent the rest of my first night filling the body bags.

I did several missions after that from the firebase. My lieutenant was a guy by the name of Kent Goolsby. We saw a lot of action together. Although there were a lot of tragic things that happened and a lot of fighting, there were also some funny things that happened. We were getting supplied one time and we were given a lot of soda, beer, and fruit. I was the

Nine. Alfred Penn Davidson

```
                DEPARTMENT OF THE ARMY
            HEADQUARTERS 4TH INFANTRY DIVISION
               APO San Francisco  96262
)ERS                                              19 August 1969
;447

         AWARD OF THE ARMY COMMENDATION MEDAL FOR HEROISM

: 320.  The following AWARD is announced:

\LFRED  186-38-0254  SPECIALIST FOUR  United States Army  HHC,
1 Inf, 4th Inf Div, APO 96265
    Army Commendation Medal with "V" Device
ion:  10 July 1969
    Republic of Vietnam
For heroism in connection with military operations against an armed
hostile force in the Republic of Vietnam.  Specialist Four Davidson
distinguished himself while serving as a Senior Medic with Company B,
1st Battalion, 8th Infantry, 4th Infantry Division.  On 10 July 1969,
Company B was moving along a ridgeline near the city of An Khe when
they came under heavy small arms fire from an enemy force of unde-
termined size.  Realizing that friendly casualties had been sustained,
Specialist Davidson rushed to the aid of his fallen comrades.  With
complete disregard for his personal safety, Specialist Davidson man-
uevered from position to position, repeatedly exposing himself to
enemy fire.  Specialist Four Davidson's selfless concern for his
fellow comrades and exemplary devotion to duty are in keeping with
the highest traditions of the military service and reflect great credit
upon himself, his unit and the United States Army.
.y.  By direction of the Secretary of the Army, under the provisions
     of AR 672-5-1.

)R THE COMMANDER:


                               GORDON J. DUQUEMIN
                               Colonel, GS
                               Chief of Staff
```

SSG Penn Davidson's Army Commendation Medal Citation.

medic and was always the guy that distributed those supplies. After the distribution, I went to sleep one night and I put some fruit inside my sleeping bag so the bugs wouldn't get all over it. I woke up in the middle of the night and something was scratching my arm. I looked up and there was an orangutan that had his arm down in my sleeping bag taking my fruit.

During the monsoon season the rains were torrential. One of the guys had an air mattress, and I blew it up to sleep on it when it was raining so hard. I went to sleep and when I woke up, I realized I had floated halfway down the mountain. There was no one around me.

We went out on patrol, and I heard something, turned around, and saw a tiger walking right down the path. The tiger was about as big as I was. On the mission we had a sergeant that had been assigned to the tanks. He was in his 40s, and he was pretty pissed off that he had gotten assigned to the infantry. We had been walking for some time and we came to a clearing and stopped to eat C rations. We had just started and a sniper started firing at us. The sniper had zoned in on the sarge. He wasn't moving very fast. Then the NVA opened up on us and rounds were flying everywhere. It was on a ridgeline near the city of An Khe and I crawled out of my position and ran to the sarge and dragged him back to cover. I received the Army Commendation Medal for my actions.

On March 24, 1969, we were sent on a suicide mission although we didn't know it at the time. The day started as several previous days with Captain DeRoos, the company commander in the base camp, sending out a platoon to check out the area. The two previous days, each platoon had been attacked about 150 meters from the base camp, having gone along

SSG Penn Davidson at Dak To, 1969.

the same ridgeline in the west along so small trails in the area. The previous day one person was killed in an area we found out later contained two regiment-size NVA base camps fresh off the Ho Chi Minh Trail. We would have the old World War II–type propeller planes come in and strafe around the perimeter at the snipers because the jets could not stay on target that long or maneuver as well. The old prop planes would make a dive at a sniper with rockets and machine guns blazing and the sniper would fire back with a single shot—bang, bang, bang. This was a regular occurrence.

Captain DeRoos decided to send two platoons out that day with our platoon in the lead and he was going to be with our platoon. Our mission was to blow a section of the Ho Chi Minh Trail with about four engineers that we had with us, in a specific area to slow the mechanized supply into Vietnam from the area where the border meets Cambodia and Laos. They did not want to send any more Phantom jets in because two had been shot down in the area by NVA dual 30 mm cannons on tracks that they would roll out from behind reinforced concrete doors, shoot, and roll back in when attacked.

Lieutenant Goolsby found out later when he was Battalion S2 intelligence officer that the NVA had a four-lane paved road with a six-inch fuel line along the side farther to the west in Cambodia and Laos to get supplies. We, on the other hand, were out of range of the nearest base for 175s or 155s (large artillery usually at a larger base camp) and at a limit for Phantom jets. We were also undersupplied and chronically low on water during the dry season. My socks and underwear had long since rotted off, and that was not something that was resupplied or deemed necessary.

SSG Penn Davidson heading out on one his many missions in Vietnam, 1969.

We decided with the two platoons and engineers to head south along the military crest of the ridgeline through the thickest underbrush we could find. The area had been defoliated along a strip north and south that bordered a strip of triple-canopy jungle farther to the west about a half a kilometer. We got out about 300 meters to the south and we heard something above us crashing through the jungle. Anticipating a major onslaught, we got down, prepared for an assault, and this herd of orangutans came swinging through the trees over the top of us. My heart rate went from 60 to 360 to 60 in one minute.

We proceeded onto a dry creek bed and then up a small embankment, turned west across a shallow flat ridgeline that went up the hill into the triple-canopy jungle, and then down into a flat valley, also in the jungle. Then we came to a well-used trail, about two or three feet wide running up the hill and down into the valley, thick with about an inch and a half of dust and a bundle of comm wire about as large as my forearm running up one side. This was not good because the landline comm wire usually would run only between two large, well-established NVA base camps. We radioed back to Captain DeRoos and told him what we had discovered. We were not at our objective yet and he suggested that we leave it alone until we had blown the road and upon returning cut out about 50 feet of it and take it off into the jungle on the way back to base camp. We left it in place, got to the objective, and set up security around the area with my platoon to the west and the other platoon to the east. We were out of water so I told Captain DeRoos that while the engineers prepped the site, we would take two men and all the canteens to what appeared to be a river about one half a kilometer farther to the west to fill up the canteens and return to the perimeter. We asked that the captain inform us and any of the men on the perimeter if the engineers were going to set off any of the shaped charges before we got back to the perimeter. We left with two men and found a beautiful clear river about 30 meters across, filled the canteens, and started our return to the perimeter.

Captain DeRoos called and said they were ready to set off the shaped charges (this is an explosive that is about eight inches in diameter and about two feet tall that has legs that space it about a foot off the ground; the bottom of the charge is an inverted conical shape like a Champagne bottle that blows a hole in the ground about 10 feet and eight inches in diameter). The side debris from the explosion would wound within about 15 to 20 meters and clear out the brush. I told him to notify my men so that we were in a safe location, and we would come back in after we heard the explosions.

Very shortly after hearing the explosions, we came back in only to find that two of the men hadn't been notified and were sitting reasonably close to one of the explosions, and blood was running out of their ears and both appeared to be shell-shocked. Captain DeRoos called in a medevac, we put them on makeshift stretchers with ponchos on sticks, chopped a landing zone in the dry bamboo with entrenching tools, and then Captain DeRoos threw out a smoke grenade to mark the position ... right into the dry bamboo we had just cut. As the medevac started to land, the smoke grenade caught the bamboo on fire and the medevac could not land. He could not wait around for another 30 minutes for us to clear another LZ, so we went about 75 meters west, cut an opening in the bamboo, and they dropped a hook to hook them out.

That is when all hell broke loose. We found out later that Captain DeRoos had ordered the rear platoon to cut out the comm wire when they crossed it, so that apparently notified the NVA regiments that there was a problem in the line and the NVA had sent contingents, apparently from both base camps along the trail, to assess the damage. They arrived just about the same time that the medevac dropped the hook and opened fire on the medevac from two sides with an amazing bruising buzz, not a rat-tat-tat. The medevac headed off dragging the hook through the bamboo, never having gotten either wounded man. I expected the hook to anchor to a tree and crash the helicopter, but it did not.

Next, the two guys who were on the stretchers decided they needed a place to hide and got up and started to congregate in a group near Captain DeRoos, all apparently in confusion. The incoming bullets were amazing with a continuous buzz. You were not able to decipher one bullet from another with their pops breaking the sound barrier as they flew past your head. The machine gunner and assistant machine gunner ran about 75 meters to the west-southwest and set up on a slight rise, behind a short rotten stump and bush to protect the flank. Most of the attack seemed to be coming from the north, east, and south, where the comm wire had been cut.

I looked out on the flat valley about five feet below and in the middle of this amazing buzz of bullets, I saw an NVA trying to flank the position. He had a starched khaki uniform, triple creased, shined boots and haircut and was walking straight at me about 50 meters out. I drew a bead on him and fired my M-16. I said that I missed, but actually, I do not know because the rifle instantly double-fed and I could not get another round in or the round out. With that one shot, also instantly, three NVA started shooting at me and the six-foot tree about arm's length away looked like a sewing machine with bullets going through and splinters raining down on me. The machine gunner and assistant machine gunner were flat on the ground as bullets broke the sound barrier next to their heads and then you heard the rifle shot. We started getting concussion grenades thrown at us with a gray cloud and minor shrapnel, one piece of which hit my lieutenant over the right eye and a small piece went into his eye. Two days later when back at base camp, I had the lieutenant have it checked out.

The circumstances of the battle were surreal. Time was expanded into slow motion. I remember looking at my pulse and thinking it was going to explode out of my wrist. I remember knowing that this was going to be the place where I died. I remember an imprint of every tree leaf and shrub around me. I remember thinking that this would be painful for my family. I remember the Lord is my shepherd Bible verse running through my head. "Yea though I walk through the valley of the shadow of death, I will fear no evil." I was not afraid. I was at peace.

I rolled up on my right side to get a grenade off my pistol belt. It was stuck. I yanked on it just as a burst of AK-47 fire went the length of where I was lying. I got the grenade off my pistol belt, pulled the pin, and threw it forward. It hit the bush in front of us and bounced back at us. My machine gunner said, "Oh my God, you have killed us." To which Lieutenant Goolsby replied, "Not yet, but you better get your head down." What we had not seen was that two NVA had crawled up into the slight depression under the bush in front of us, and when the grenade went off, it killed one instantly and the other one ran about 10 feet before his insides came out. I did not have any more grenades and the machine gunner said, "Hey, we better do that again." After that the entire perimeter was dead silent.

Apparently, our being out 75 meters from the main unit made them think we were a larger force than we were. There was dead silence for several minutes. Then I heard someone from the main unit say, "I think they killed Lieutenant Goolsby." There were several more calls to the lieutenant, but he was not saying anything, and he did not have a radio. Then someone said, "We better throw more grenades out that way." And Lieutenant Goolsby said, "Dammit, you better not." Then they said, "We will lay down some fire and you can come back in." They did and we did.

There were wounded and killed back in the main group. Captain DeRoos said, "Take the platoon and go up the hill, and we will carry the wounded." Lieutenant Goolsby asked if the captain was going to call in artillery before they got there because that was where the comm wire was running.

We got the worst of it when guys in the trees that we hadn't seen started dropping grenades on us. We ran into the outpost of one of the two regimental NVA base camps that we happened to be between, again not knowing that at the time, but suspecting it after seeing the comm wire that was running along the dusty trail down into the valley, which Captain DeRoos ordered cut after the platoon passed against Lieutenant Goolsby's request, rather than waiting until we finished blowing the section of the Ho Chi Ming Trail. When we did not get artillery on the top of the hill as Lieutenant Goolsby requested from Captain DeRoos, that's when all hell broke loose.

During the fight, Larry Conklin was hit several times and was losing a lot of blood. For a short time, the firing had stopped. I hooked up a serum albumin to give him a blood transfusion. The NVA who were in the trees dropping concussion grenades dropped one between me and Lieutenant Goolsby and blew my pack to pieces. It looked like a geyser of pills blown into the air.

SSG Penn Davidson in the bush in Vietnam, 1969.

It blew me back against some trees and I hurt my back. I finally got back to Conklin, and he died in my arms. That has haunted me to this day. He should have not died. I have had nightmares for years over it. I took a hit of morphine for my back injury, and we went farther up the hill into the ambush. Then the radio operator had a concussion grenade hit him and blow him through a bush. We thought he was dead, but he stood up and said, "No, I am fine, but the radio is not working."

We moved back down the hill to a defensive position, not realizing the captain had already taken two-thirds of the platoon and moved farther back down the hill without telling us. Another grenade dropped and hit the radio operator on the back of the leg, which did not appear to bleed. It looked like a piece of steak, and he took off running somehow as another wave of grenades came in. One grenade threw me up in the crotch of a small tree on my back with my head angled down the hill. Our point man was blown on top of me the same way. I could not get up or move, but another grenade hit the point man in the stomach and unfortunately removed all of his insides as he slowly rotated off me. I was looking at his membrane-covered backbone and ribs with nothing else inside his body, but again there was no appreciable blood as he floated off in what appeared to be slow motion and, with a guttural rattle, disappeared into the brush. And then we were at the top of the hill alone and did not see the point man or anyone else.

We crisscrossed the ridge trying to pick up anybody and get them down the hill until we could get some artillery, which never came until late in the evening for our night defensive position about 100 meters down the hill. I heard about five people chamber rounds as we emerged through the brush with relief on both sides that I had caught up to the platoon and neither of us had shot each other.

We found Captain DeRoos and asked what his plan was in a circle of about six people, and he was so nervous he fired his M-16 into the ground between Lieutenant Goolsby and the radio operator, and the radio operator said, "Sir, if you don't get me away from this SOB, I am going to shoot him myself." At which time Captain DeRoos started running down the hill. None of us could hear much of anything except ringing in our ears at that point.

It was an easy path to follow as every leaf, branch, and twig was covered with blood waist high down. A bright red path through a bright green jungle with the sun shining at the far end of the path. A surreal sight. We made our way to the front and stopped by a redheaded guy who happened to be in our platoon, and we were standing in the very spot where we had had the first shooting battle that morning in the valley, but that is another story because I was nearly killed there only three times rather than the 10 times up on the hill. We knew where we were. We went over to a dry bed, set up a perimeter, and tried to call in artillery on the hill and the other NVA camp below us from the base camp. The battalion commander answered and said, "Can't talk now, under attack," as NVA artillery blew the sandbags off the TOC.

The next morning, we had helicopters come in to pick us up. I had gotten separated from the unit and was hiding in some elephant grass as I could hear the NVA all around. I could hear them talking. As the choppers were loading, they came under mortar fire. As one helicopter took off and hit the tree line, the NVA opened up and Captain DeRoos was wounded in the leg. Lieutenant Goolsby was in another chopper. They were receiving hundreds of rounds and it shut off the motor to the helicopter's rotor and the two pilots looked at each other like this would not end well. They threw the chopper into auto rotate and disengaged the rotor and the chopper began to glide just above the tops of the trees at the same angle as the hill. Lieutenant Goolsby later recalled that he laughed because he had come so close to being killed many times the two days before and now he was going to die in a helicopter crash. Just as they were about to crash into the mountain on the other side of the valley, the left pilot hit some magic switch with his right hand in the middle of the roof after frantically trying all sorts of other switches and we heard a chunk, then another chunk, and then the motor kicked in and an angel reached down and picked up the chopper seconds before it was going to crash and they flew back to the base.

Several other guys and I were left behind. We were all separated from each other and all hiding from the NVA. I hid in the elephant grass for three days. I could hear the NVA several times talking. They were fairly close to me, but I hid well in the tall grass. After three days I never heard them anymore and I came out of the grass and made my way back to the base camp. I had been MIA for three days.

I remember going on a mission with the company and we were gone for about two weeks, and we were humping through the jungle. The lieutenant kept looking at the map because he knew where we were going. We had the lieutenant first, then me and the radio operator, in that order. Everybody else was behind us. I always wanted to be in the front of the pack. I always wanted to know where we were going. We had run out of water, and we were worn out when we came upon a small pond. I can just remember it was clear water. I can't remember if there was a waterfall or not. Everyone was filling their canteens and I was passing out iodine pills to put in their canteens, but most of the guys had already drunk by that time. Anyway, several of us, including me, took our clothes off and jumped in the pond, a dumb-ass thing to do. While we were in there, a sniper started shooting at us. I hurried out of the pond and jumped into my clothes and picked up my rucksack. It saved my life because I took a round into it. We all took off running and ended up in an intense firefight. I helped this segreant that had taken a round in his calf. All the meat of his leg was gone and all you could see was the bone. The firefight continued, and we were able to get the sergeant evacuated out of the area on a chopper. I loaded him and several others wounded throughout the day under fire and was awarded my second Silver Star.

After several months of being in the field, we were supposed to be assigned to a different duty other than being in the bush. When my time was up in the bush, I found out I was being assigned to Graves Registration. I was really pissed off at that because that's where you go in and put body parts together. I refused to go and the captain said he was going to give me a court-martial if I didn't go, so I went to see the battalion commander and the battalion commander understood and made sure I didn't have to take that assignment.

I then volunteered to do medevacs. I had several missions. I basically filled in for guys. I was in three helicopter crashes. Two of them, we were

HEADQUARTERS 4TH INFANTRY DIVISION
APO San Francisco 96262

ERS   August 1969
5585

AWARD OF THE SILVER STAR

C 320. The following AWARD is announced:

ALFRED C 186-38-0254 SPECIALIST FOUR United States Army, Co B,
h Inf, 4th Inf Div, APO 96265
: Silver Star
ion: 25 March 1969
: Republic of Vietnam
For gallantry in action while engaged in military operations against an armed hostile force in the Republic of Vietnam. Specialist Four Davidson distinguished himself while serving as a Medic with Company B, 1st Battalion, 8th Infantry, 4th Infantry Division. On 25 March 1969, Specialist Davidson's unit had the mission of interdicting an enemy supply route in the Plei Trap Valley area. As the lead platoon of the two platoon size friendly unit moved forward they came under intense fire from an unknown size enemy force. In the initial contact, several personnel were severely wounded. With complete disregard for his perso safety, Specialist Davidson moved forward from his position in the rear to aid his comrades in the forward elements. Placing himself in the direct line of fire, he carried wounded personnel to safety on several occasions. As the friendly unit continued to advance on the enemy they again came under intense enemy fire from well-entrenched troops occupying the high ground. Again, without regard for his personal safety, Specialist Davidson advanced under a hail of small arms, automatic weapons and grenade fire to treat the wounded. When an enemy grenade exploded near him, wounding him and throwing him down a steep hill, Specialist Davidson stood up undaunted and, with pistol in hand, attempted to move up the hill. He continued to provide covering fire for the wounded until he was ordered to receive medical attention by the company commander. Specialist Four Davidson's personal bravery, outstanding performance and exemplary devotion to duty are in keeping with the highest traditions of the military service and reflect great credit upon himself, his unit and the United States Army.
ty: By direction of the President, under the provisions of the Act of Congress, approved 9 July 1918.

SSG Penn Davidson's Silver Star Citation.

shot down and the third was an accident. The first one, we were coming into Firebase 29 and we were setting down to take some wounded out that had been there for a day or so and some sappers were in the wire, and they had some kind of weapon and fired at the helicopter and there was explosion like a fireball at the back of the helicopter. We crashed and went on one side. Gunships were called in and they provided us support and protection and about 30 minutes later another chopper came in and rescued us. All of us—the pilot, copilot, gunner, and myself—made it out.

The second one, there was a C Company unit that was pinned down in the jungle and was taking heavy fire from all sides and we were called in to take out all the wounded. We circled several times to get in and finally had a small area where we could land, but before we could land, we were hit by small arms fire. We went on a spiral and went down and hit hard and then went to one side. I got a head injury and was all scratched up. One pilot broke his leg. The ground unit helped us all out and we stayed with them overnight. I worked on several wounded guys in the unit during that time. I had one wounded guy that died overnight. The next day we were evacuated by helicopter while the unit stayed and finished their mission.

The third one, we went in to pick up some wounded and while we were didn't take on any fire at that time. They loaded three wounded soldiers, and we took off. One of the wounded was hurt pretty bad, the other two not so bad. We took off and as we started flying out, I smelled fuel. I looked out and there was fuel pouring out of the fuel tank. The pilot had set the helicopter down in a bamboo area and a piece of bamboo had punctured the gas tank. We were all yelling at the pilot about the leak, and he said we had enough fuel to get back to the base camp. About a quarter of a mile from the base camp, we ran out of fuel and the helicopter just started spinning around and around until we slammed into the ground. We all walked away from it bruised and banged up.

Besides medevacs, I also worked with the pacification program. It was a program to help rural Vietnamese with health care and building infrastructure. We also trained the ARVN, and I trained many ARVN medics. On one of the missions we were on, we found a large rice cache. The commanding officer made us haul the bundles of rice down the mountain to a nearby village. After a few days of that, a buddy and I decided that it was too much work. When no one was looking, my buddy took his cigarette lighter and threw it in the rice cache and it caught on fire and burned up. We didn't have to carry any more rice.

When I returned from Vietnam on Christmas Eve, I got to the airport, and we got as far as Pittsburgh and it was snowing so hard I had to go the rest of the way to Harrisburg by train. When I was in the airport, I think I was called everything possible. When I got off the train in Harrisburg, the first thing, I took my uniform off and shoved it in a trash can. I didn't want anybody to know that I was a Vietnam veteran. I stayed in the train station on Christmas Eve and Christmas Day by myself. I drank heavy while I was there. The day after Christmas I took a cab over to the Chevrolet dealership. I had a pocketful of money and I bought myself a brand-new Chevy Super Sport.

After I got out of the Army, no one wanted to hire me. I finally got a job as manager trainee in a family restaurant. I worked there for about a year. I became a manger of a steak house and then later became the regional manager for over 60 steak houses. Then after I did that, I went to

SSG Penn Davidson (front, center) and ARVN medic trainees at Dak To, 1969.

work for a company called ARA in sports arenas and stadiums. It was a company that provided food in those places. In 1980, I was providing the food served for the Winter Olympics. I was there for the hockey game.

Then I moved to Denver, Colorado. I ran 14 ski areas, including Aspen ski area. Did that for a year or so. During that time, I went through two marriages. Neither of them worked out. Then I moved to my sister's on a farm in Delaware. I stayed with my sister for a while. Later on, I became a manager of the Hilton Hotel. I worked my way up to vice president. I worked in a hotel in Huntsville, Alabama, and my boss was Alan Shepard, the astronaut who owned the hotel.

In 2006 I started having problems with PTSD. I was just mentally screwed up. I went to the VA for help. It took me about 10 years to realize I had needed help. I went through a couple of wives with the PTSD and being all messed up. With one wife we burned all my medals in the fireplace one night. I was a mess at the time. Now I have been married to my

Penn Davidson with his daughter Shana at the Vietnam Wall Memorial in Washington, D.C., 1992.

present wife for 40 years. I did the counseling, took the drugs, and got myself straightened out. I ended up selling all of my partnerships in the hotels and I retired. In 2007 we moved to Orange Beach, Alabama, where I live now. My wife, Jeanne, and I love to fish and enjoy the beach.

I've been to the wall in Washington several times. I have a photo of me holding my little girl and she is pointing at a name on the wall. That little girl is my daughter Shana. She asked me if I knew any of the people on the wall. There are 17 names on that wall, and I was one of four that survived. The wall has great meaning for me.

When we were living in Washington, we applied for a VA loan. I was told that I could go to the office downtown and get the loan quicker. We went down there, and short story was that I couldn't get the loan because they had reported me as killed in action in Vietnam. The true story was that I was an MIA for three and a half days and I hid out in the elephant grass while the NVA walked all around me, and I went from MIA to the Army declaring me KIA. Then I had to prove I was still alive.

We spent a lot of time in the Mountain Yard villages. One day we went into a village and there was a teenager all shot up and I patched him up. Got him out on a helicopter and saved his life. The Mountain Yard chief gave me a crossbow with arrows made out of bamboo and I still have them till this day.

I am fortunate I had three children. My oldest daughter, Kristyna Eagle, is a guidance counselor at a high school. I have a son, Mark, that is a CEO at a high-tech company, and my other daughter, Shana, is a registered nurse. I have a granddaughter, Julia Davidson, who is now at the U.S. Navy Academy at Annapolis. She is carrying on the military tradition in the family.

Most medics spent their time in Vietnam handing out medication. Besides the wounded and killed, I had to make sure the soldiers took malaria pills and had to give my share of penicillin shots for venereal disease. I spent a lot of time trimming the calluses off the nasty feet because we went days and weeks and months with no fresh socks. I treated a number of heat strokes from climbing up and down the mountains. I felt like I was a little bit of a shrink dealing with some of the emotional problems.

I carried an M-79 while in the bush, which is unusual for medics. It was just something I wanted to do. I loved my men. I did take the best care I could for them. I have never considered myself a hero because I lost too many men. I just served and did the best I could and did the best job I knew how. Kent Goolsby was the bravest soldier and officer I have ever known. In October 2021, Lieutenant Goolsby was buried in Arlington National Cemetery with full honors. Kent died from the Agent Orange he was exposed to in Vietnam. I am proud of being a part of the 4th Army Division and I am proud of being a Vietnam veteran.

Appendix A
In Memory

Lieutenant Robert Kent Goolsby
1st Battalion, 8th Regiment, Company B, 4th Marine Division
August 14, 1944–October 5, 2021

Lieutenant Robert K. Goolsby was Staff Sergeant Medic Penn Davidson's platoon leader. They served together on the operation of March 24, 1969, at the Ho Chi Minh Trail. After they were discharged from the service, for 50 years on March 24 they always sent each other a birthday card. They always considered it to be their second birthday because both should have died that day. It was the day they were reborn. As Staff Sergeant Davidson said, "Lieutenant Goolsby is the bravest soldier and the finest officer I ever served with in the Army." Lieutenant Goolsby's death was a result of exposure to Agent Orange.

Robert Kent Goolsby passed away on Tuesday, October 5, 2021. Born August 14, 1944, in Lynchburg, Virginia, to the late Robert "Bill" Beverly and Beulah (Winebarger) Goolsby, Kent graduated from Boonsboro High School in Boonsboro, Virginia, and went on to Virginia Polytechnic Institute and State University, obtaining a degree in architecture and a master's degree in urban planning.

Kent served in the U.S. Army, rising to the rank of 1st Lieutenant. During that time in the Army, Kent served as an officer in the prestigious Old Guard tied to the White House and Arlington Cemetery. He later served as a platoon leader in Vietnam, earning numerous medals including the Bronze Star and Silver Star. The Silver Star, the Army's third-highest honor, was awarded to Kent in 1969 for distinguishing himself by advancing under heavy enemy fire to take out a sniper position with a well-placed grenade. For those who knew Kent, this would come as no surprise.

Returning from Vietnam in 1969 was no picnic, but over the years Kent took great pride in his service and reconnected with many Vietnam veterans from the 1st Battalion, 8th Infantry in which he served. Kent's admiration for the military lives on through the monument he designed for the Korean War Memorial in Mint Hill, which was the first memorial in North Carolina devoted solely to Korean War veterans.

In 1972, Kent moved to Charlotte, North Carolina, to pursue a job in architecture. It's also where he met his wife, Patricia (Pat). Married on October 5, 1973, they would have celebrated their 48th wedding anniversary this year.

During Kent's career as an architect, he worked at several firms in the Charlotte area, serving as a principal at J.H. Pease Architecture before starting his own firm. He loved being an architect and continued to practice until his death.

Throughout his life, Kent found his greatest joy in family and the many friendships he nurtured over the years. He was enormously proud of his two daughters, who grew up to embody the same kindness, courage, and can-do spirit that defined Kent. Kent always loved sharing his knowledge and inspiring curiosity in the next generation. In his mind, this was a "job well done." Affectionately known as "Grand dude," Kent loved spending time with his grandchildren going to the beach, taking flashlight walks at night, swinging in the hammock, and any other silly things he or they could think of.

Kent loved traveling throughout the world, as well as enjoyed his many trips back to his hometown of Lynchburg, where he stayed connected to family and many lifelong friends. No matter what or where, Kent was always up for the next adventure.

Described by his friends as the quintessential Southern gentleman, Kent was kind, thoughtful, and eager to help people however he could. He was a man of service. No matter what needed to be done, occasions to be celebrated, Kent always showed up. He was a man of many talents—a true Renaissance man. Whatever Kent didn't know how to do, he learned how to do. It is almost impossible to sum up a life so well lived.

SP 4 Larry J. Conklin

1st Battalion, 8th Regiment, Company B, 4th Infantry Division

Panel 28W018

On the day Larry Conklin was wounded, Staff Sergeant Davidson was tending to Conklin's wounds. Davidson was administering a blood transfusion on Conklin when a concussion grenade dropped near them. Staff Sergeant Davidson was blown against a tree, injuring his back. Nevertheless and disregarding his own injuries, he crawled back to Conklin attempting to save his life. Conklin died in Davidson's arms. To this day, Staff Sergeant Davidson has been haunted by Larry Conklin's death. As Davidson said, "He just wasn't supposed to die." Staff Sergeant Davidson did everything he could for his fellow soldier. But, as all combat medics know, they never talk about all those they saved. They are always haunted by the ones they didn't save. The second award was received for actions during their battle that day.

Silver Star Citation (1st Award)

Awarded for actions during the Vietnam War

The President of the United States of America, authorized by Act of Congress July 9, 1918 (amended by an act of July 25, 1963), takes pleasure in presenting the Silver Star to Private First Class Larry James Conklin (ASN:US-52969184), United States Army, for gallantry in action in connection with military operations against an armed hostile force in the Republic of Vietnam. Private First Class Conklin distinguished himself while serving as a Pointman with Company B, 1st Battalion, 8th Infantry Regiment, 4th Infantry Division. On 13 October 1968, Private First Class Conklin and several of his comrades were on a patrol near Dak To when they were engaged by the enemy force. Rolling forward, Private First Class Conklin engaged the enemy with devastating fire, thwarting their attack temporarily. When the enemy regrouped and initiated a second assault he charged them firing his automatic weapon and hurling grenades with such accuracy that the enemy ran for cover. Then as a thunderstorm started, Private First Class Conklin attempted to repair the damaged radio to establish communications with his firebase.

Attempting to replace the severed band receiver, he tied the wires and spliced them, but received an inaudible transmission as the splice worked loose. Twice attempting to make a secure splice, Private First Class Conklin bit down on the wires with his teeth and held the bare splice in his hands despite the severe shocks he was receiving. Finally establishing communications, he called for and directed mortar fire on the fleeing enemy troops. Then moving to the aid of a severely wounded comrade, Private First Class Conklin splinted the man's shattered leg and comforted him until an evacuation helicopter arrived. Private First Class Conklin's exceptional courage, perseverance and exemplary devotion to duty are in keeping with the highest traditions of the military service and reflect great upon himself, his unit and the United States Army.

General Orders: Headquarters, 4th Infantry Division, General Orders No. 6110 (November 28, 1968)

Silver Star 2nd Award

Awarded for actions during the Vietnam War

The President of the United States of America, authorized by Act of Congress July 9, 1918 (amended by an act of July 25, 1963), takes pride in presenting a Bronze Oak Leaf Cluster in lieu of a second Award of the Silver Star (Posthumously) to Specialist Fourth Class Larry James Conklin (ASN:US-52969184) United States Army, for gallantry in action in connection with military operations against an armed hostile force in the Republic of Vietnam. At approximately 0900 hours, 23 March 1969, Company B, 1st Battalion, 8th Infantry Regiment, 4th Infantry Division, while returning from a platoon-size mission west of Kon Tum City, made contact with an enemy force of undetermined strength. Specialist Fourth Class Conklin was the squad leader for the first squad, which was the lead element at the time. Realizing the main element was in danger, he began deploying his squad to positions covering the flanks. With complete disregard for his own personal safety, he remained standing in open terrain, continually exposed to a barrage of hostile grenade and rifle fire in an attempt to pinpoint the enemy emplacement. Then, aided by the intense base of fire he was directing at the enemy, he succeeded in maneuvering his men to positions affording them better protection. While laying down the covering fire, he was mortally wounded. His personal bravery, superb leadership and exemplary devotion to duty are in keeping with the highest traditions of the military service and reflect great credit upon himself, his unit, and the United States Army.

General Orders, Headquarters, 4th Infantry Division, General Orders No. 1040 (April 7, 1969)

Appendix B
Vietnam Facts and Statistics

1. Many believe that President John F. Kennedy was the first to send advisers to South Vietnam. However, he inherited the situation from earlier administrations. President Harry S. Truman was the first to send advisers, in 1950, to all levels of the South Vietnamese military. In 1954, when the French left Vietnam, Dwight Eisenhower continued to train the South Vietnamese troops in Vietnam.
2. In 1964, President Lyndon Johnson claimed that the USS *Maddox* and the USS *Turner* were attacked by the North Vietnamese Navy. As a result, he was able to get the Gulf of Tonkin Resolution passed in Congress. Secretary of Defense Robert McNamara testified three years later before Congress that the incident never happened.
3. The Vietnam War lasted 20 years, from 1955 to 1975.
4. The war killed more than three million people, including two million civilians.
5. North Vietnam sent 1.1 million troops to South Vietnam, while the United States and South Vietnam had nearly five million.
6. Vietnam was the most heavily bombed country in history, with more than seven million tons of bombs.
7. The war was fought in North and South Vietnam, Cambodia, and Laos.
8. It's a myth that Vietnam was fought by draftees. Only about 25 percent of those who fought in Vietnam were drafted.
9. Another myth is that the Vietnam War was fought by the poorly educated. The fact is that 79 percent of those who fought in Vietnam were high school graduates or higher.
10. Kim Phuc, the Vietnamese girl shown in the famous photo running down the road nude and burned by napalm, was not hit by the United States. The South Vietnamese Air Force dropped the bombs while supporting an ARVN unit in the area.
11. A total of 2,709,918 Americans served in the Vietnam War.
12. Of them, 240 men were awarded the Medal of Honor.
13. There were 23,214 service members who were 100 percent disabled; 5,283 lost limbs, and 1,081 lost more than one limb.

14. Sixty-one percent of U.S. service members killed in Vietnam were younger than 21; 11,465 were younger than 20; and 17,539 were married.

15. The average age of someone killed in action during the Vietnam war was 23.1 years.

16. As of 2017, 1,611 U.S. service members were still unaccounted for: 1,258 in Vietnam, 297 in Laos, 49 in Cambodia, and seven in China.

17. Eighty-seven percent of Americans hold Vietnam veterans in high esteem. Eighty-five percent of Vietnam veterans made successful transitions back to civilian life, 97 percent were honorably discharged, 91 percent were glad they served, and 74 percent say they would do it again.

18. It's a myth that infantrymen served a lot more time in battle during World War II than in Vietnam. The fact is that the average infantryman in the Pacific during World War II served about 40 days in combat in four years. In Vietnam, the average was 240 days in one year.

19. Although the casualty rate was higher in World War II than in Vietnam, the amputee rate for veterans was 300 times higher in Vietnam than World War II.

20. Another myth is that the average age in Vietnam was 19 for servicemen. It was actually 22. In World War II, it was 26.

21. Protesters often falsely claimed that the draft unfairly targeted minorities during the Vietnam War. In fact, over 80 percent of draftees were white and 10–15 percent were African Americans, which was proportionate to the overall population at the time.

22. A federal study found nearly 300,000 Vietnam veterans suffer from daily health problems as a result of their experiences in the Vietnam War.

23. Although we lost the Vietnam War, the United States of America military armed forces in Vietnam never lost a battle.

Vietnam Wall Memorial

The Vietnam Veterans Memorial (often known as The Wall) represents U.S. armed forces members who served and died in the Vietnam War from 1955 to 1975. The monument located in Washington, D.C., was designed by American architect Maya Lin. As a senior undergraduate at Yale University, Lin entered a nationwide competition sponsored by the Vietnam Veterans Memorial Fund. Her design was selected out of 1,400 submissions. The monument was dedicated on November 13, 1982.

The wall was designed with a polished black granite V-shaped wall inscribed with the names of 58,313 men and women (nurses) who were killed or went missing in action in the Vietnam War. One hundred of those names are of Canadian citizens. The names are arranged in the order in which they died, and within each date they are alphabetized.

The first person killed in Vietnam was Richard B. Fitzgibbon from North Weymouth, Massachusetts, on June 8, 1956. His name is listed along with his son Lance Corporal Richard B. Fitzgibbon III, killed September 7, 1965.

There are three sets of fathers and sons on the wall.

Of Americans killed, 12 were 17 years old; five were 16 years old; the youngest was PFC Dan Bullock, who was 15 years old.

There are 31 sets of brothers on the wall.

Of the 244 soldiers who received the Medal of Honor in the Vietnam War, 153 are on the wall.

A total of 997 soldiers were killed during their first day in Vietnam.

Beallsville, Ohio, population 475, lost six servicemen.

West Virginia had the highest casualty rate per population of any state, with 711 killed in action.

The most casualties in a single day was 245 killed in action on January 31, 1968.

The month with the most casualties was May 1968, with 2,415.

Three friends from Midvale, Utah, lived within three blocks of each other, one on Fifth Street, one on Sixth Street, and the third on Seventh Street. They all went to Vietnam together. In 1967, one was killed on the fourth anniversary of the John F. Kennedy assassination. Within 24 hours, the second one was killed on Thanksgiving Day. The third died on Pearl Harbor Day 1967.

A group of nine young men from the mining town of Morenci, Arizona, joined the Marine Corps together. Their first day of duty was Independence Day 1966. Only three returned.

Index

Alaska 68
Anchorage, Alaska 72
Andrews, Bruce 128, 129
An Khe, Vietnam 29, 36, 38, 44, 66, 154
Archer, Tom 57
Arlington National Cemetery 150
Armendarig, Patrick 76
Armstrong, Neil 120
Ashau Valley, Vietnam 84, 92, 95

B Company, 2nd-501, 101st Airborne Infantry 71, 73, 74, 81, 86
Bahle, Ted 56
Baldwin, Bob 76, 80
Bangkok 24
Bargatze, Landis 132
Barnes, James E. 126, 127, 129, 130, 131, 133, 135
Barretto, Jorge 111
Battle of the Bulge 18
Bein Hoa, Vietnam 23, 24, 73
Beverly, Robert 167, 168
Boyd, F.B. 86
Bryson, Paco 143
Bullock, Dan 172
Burel, Lloyd 47
Butts, Robert 76

Caldwell, Archibald 41, 42, 47, 52
Calhoun, Pat 58
Cam Ranh Bay, Vietnam 6, 15, 61, 63, 71, 72, 136, 147
Cambodia 24, 142, 155, 170, 171
Camp Eagle 96, 116
Camp Evans 109
Camp Radcliff 36, 37, 38, 57, 64, 65
Camp Sally 109
Canada 18
Carrara, Wayne 100
Casey, Ben 35
Central Highlands, Vietnam 136, 146
Charlotte, North Carolina 168

Chu Lai, Vietnam 6
Clark Air Force Base 28
Conklin, Larry 159, 168, 169
Connors, Wendell 132
Corbin, Cherry 91

Dak To, Vietnam 30, 36, 37, 39, 40, 42, 43, 128, 130, 131, 132, 134, 137, 139, 140, 143, 145, 146, 152, 164
Dalegowski, Gary 30
Dallas, Texas 106, 118
Danang, Vietnam 74, 76, 92, 96, 117
Davidson, Alfred Penn 150, 151, 152, 153, 154, 155, 157, 164, 159, 161, 162, 163, 164, 165, 167, 168, 170, 171
Delaware 150, 164
Denver, Colorado 164
Detroit, Michigan 76
de Varona Donna de 49
Dongo, Bob 70

85th Evac Hospital 120, 121
82nd Airborne 73
Europe 118

1st Battalion, 8th Infantry Regiment, 4th Infantry Division 128, 136, 150, 151, 167
Fisher, Dale 76
Fitzgibbon 111, Richard B. 171
Flint, Michigan 143
Flory, Leo 71, 75, 77, 81, 89, 91, 93, 95, 97, 99, 101, 103, 104, 105
Fort Bliss, Texas 17
Fort Bragg 150
Fort Dix 19
Fort Hood 127, 136
Fort Jackson 6
Fort Lewis 148
Fort Meade 107, 118
Fort Myer 151
Fort Ord 118, 120, 136
Fort Polk 127

Index

Fort Riley, Kansas 136
Fort Sam Houston 6, 7, 19, 28, 107, 127, 136
4th Battalion, 21st Infantry Division 5
4th Infantry Division 28
Frazier, Albert 130
Furlough, Dave 33, 36

Glendale, California 149
Global, George 46
Goolsby, Beulah (Winebarger) 167
Goolsby, Kent 53, 54, 157, 167
Graney, Pierce T. 96
Green, Jimmy 76, 103
Greenville, Texas 132
Gulf of Tonkin, Vietnam 105, 170
Gundagno, Michael 5, 7, 8, 9, 11, 13, 15, 18
Guns, Clyde 86

Hadley, William 130
Hallums, James 83
Harrisburg, Pennsylvania 163
Hartison, Bob 31, 32
Hawaii 28, 48
Hendricks, Jimmy 30, 31
Herrin, James 57
Hetly, Frank 76
HHC 1st, 502nd, 101st Airborne Division 106
Hilly, Frank 76
Ho Chi Minh Trail, Vietnam 132, 142, 155, 159
Hue, Vietnam 71, 76, 80, 89, 121
Holden, Willie 142
Hope, Bob 124
Hopkins, Perry 57
Horn, Pete 55
Howard, Matt 31, 32
Hubbard, Raymond 28, 29, 31, 35, 37, 44, 45, 47, 48, 51, 53, 55, 57, 58, 59, 63, 65, 66, 67, 68, 69
Hudson, Joe 76
Hue, Vietnam 71, 76, 80, 89, 121
Huntsville, Alabama 165

I Corps (Vietnam) 15, 121, 124
Ia Drang Valley, Vietnam 128, 132
Indiana, Chesterton 50

Johns, Jackie 76

Kansas 20
Kates, John 121
Keddie, William, Jr. 106, 107, 109, 111, 112, 114, 115, 116, 117, 118
Kennedy, John F. 170, 172
King, Martin Luther, Jr. 150

Koffman, Bill 96
Kontrabecki, Al 76
Korea 107
Krantscheid, David 97
Krenger, Rick 48, 50, 55

Laos 80, 130, 132, 155, 170
Leary, Pat 76
Little, Don 36, 46
Locklear, Carl 51
Long Bien, Vietnam 29
Los Angeles, California 128
Lynchburg, Virginia 167
Lyons, Joe 129
Lysne, Gary 54, 56, 60

Maag, John M. 136, 137, 138, 139, 141, 143, 145, 147, 149
USS *Maddox* 170
Manhatton, New York 76
Marsolik, Steve 56
Maryland 118
McCloud Air Force Base 16
McCouan, Irvin 76
Midvale, Utah 172
Morenci, Arizona 172
Murphy, Audie 10

Nagel, Carl 65
New York City 69, 151
Niagara Falls 76
Noland, John 42, 70
Norris, Jim 56
North, Steve 48
North Weymouth, Massachusetts 171

Oakland 20, 24, 28, 29
Ohio, Beallsville 172
Oklahoma, Tulsa 91
197th Medical Detachment, 212th Aviation Battalion, 1st Aviation Brigade 18
173rd Airborne 73, 134
Orange Beach, Alabama 165

Paris Peace Treaty 149
Pastor, Richard 18, 19, 21, 22, 23, 24, 25
Penney, Richard 138
Perfume River 93
Phu Bai, Vietnam 121
Pittsburg, Pennsylvania 163
Pleiku, Vietnam 29, 61, 66, 127, 130, 136, 146
Pohl Bridge 92

Quang Nai Province, Vietnam 6, 12, 15
Quang Tri, Vietnam 76

Index

Reinheimer, David 76
Roland, Erin 36, 48, 50

St. Louis, Missouri 76, 120
San Antonio, Texas 132
San Fernando, California 143
Scala, Joe 46
Settler, Glenn 48, 52, 70
Simmons, Bruce 65
Sinatra, Nancy 142, 143
South Carolina 145
Steedley, Homer 52, 54, 55, 56, 57
Sydney, Australia 61, 62, 63

Thomas, Frank 31, 70
Thou Thin Province, Vietnam 89
Transition to Duty 105
Trask, Larry 76
Travis Air Force Base 109
Truman, Harry S. 170
Tubbs, Gordon 130
Tulsa, Oklahoma 91
USS *Turner* 170

University of New Hampshire 18
USO 83

Vermeesch, Wes 57

Wagnisk, Jim 46
Waite, Mel 76
Wake Island 28, 109
Wakefield 76
Walker, Glenda 62
Wallace, George 118
Washington, D.C. 127, 151, 166
Welch, Garry 76
Whitlow, Billy 56
Williams, L. Dwayne 120, 121, 122, 123, 124, 125
World War II 127, 135, 171

Yamashita, Ted 42, 70
Yeaguine, Ruben 112
Yucota, Japan 71

www.ingramcontent.com/pod-product-compliance
Ingram Content Group UK Ltd.
Pitfield, Milton Keynes, MK11 3LW, UK
UKHW042015140426
5217IPUK00015B/1183